Going to
SEED

Edible Plants of the Southwest
& How to Prepare Them

Written and Illustrated by
KAHANAH FARNSWORTH

Botanical Consultant
GWEN HULBERT

ANCIENT CITY PRESS
SANTA FE, NEW MEXICO

"And God said, Behold, I have given you every
herb bearing seed, which is upon the face of all the earth,
and every tree, in which is the fruit of a tree yielding seed;
to you it shall be for meat."
—
Genesis 1:29

Original book design by John Cole
Revised book design by Kathleen Sparkes, White Hart Design
Cover design by Janice St. Marie

Library of Congress Cataloging-in-Publication Data

Farnsworth, Kahanah, 1946–
  Going to Seed : finding, identifying, and preparing edible plants of the
Southwest / by Kahanah Farnsworth; botanical consultant, Gwen Hulbert.
      p. cm.
  Includes bibliographical references and index.
  ISBN 1-58096-006-5 (pbk. : alk. paper)
  1. Wild plants, Edible—Southwest, New. 2. Cookery (wild foods)
I. Title.
QK98.5.U6F27   1999
581.6'32'0979 — dc21   98-55087
                                                                          CIP
Printed in Canada

DISCLAIMER

Please use common sense and consult a
qualified instructor if there is any question about which plants
are edible. If any plants are being used singly or in combination as medicine, contact a health care practitioner before
using them. The author, publisher, and bookseller assume no
liability for the misuse of plants by the reader.

CONTENTS

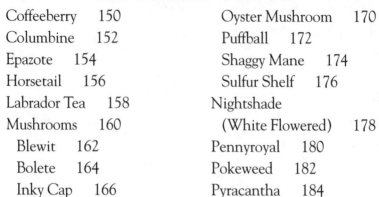

INTRODUCTION

oing to Seed is a reader-friendly field guide to edible, questionable, and poisonous plants and mushrooms which were selected for their availability and easy recognition. All grow in the Southwest, and most can be found scattered throughout the United States and other countries. Delicious, healthy recipes are included for edible and questionable plants. All chapters contain drawings, descriptions, and interesting facts. Whenever possible, Native American and medicinal uses are given. If there is any chance of confusing one plant with another, the differences between the two are clearly stated. Photos are included as well as a plant substitution appendix and an illustrated glossary. In addition, other common edible plants and recipes and poisonous plants not covered in *Going to Seed* can be found in my first book, *A Taste of Nature*.

Discovering and identifying plants ranks somewhere between detective work and treasure hunting. Creating delicious recipes and finding new uses for plants is "icing on the cake." Please remember that we are gatherers not destroyers. Do not pick rare or endangered plants. Look for prosperous plants growing in groups, and only pick as much as you can use. Watch out for chemicals, polluted water, and car fumes. Often there are choice plants growing in parks. Do not hesitate to ask a ranger if you can pick a few. They often permit this once they realize that you are responsible and respect park regulations.

As you use this book, remember that there is no such thing as the exact size of a plant or the precise season in which it grows. Plants are influenced by many factors: their geographic location, the altitude and climate where they grow, how near they are to water, and if they are shaded or in full sun. Consequently, although the statistics and seasons given in this book are generally accurate, there are always exceptions. For example, plants which are available during late winter in southern California may not appear until several months later at a higher altitude or in a northern climate.

Kahanah Farnsworth is a teacher and outdoor educator who has worked as a volunteer for the San Diego Natural History Museum leading nature hikes. Being an avid cook, she loves to experiment with natural ingredients. Her interests include hiking, camping, and painting. She resides in southern California near San Diego, and is the author of the highly-acclaimed edible plant guide A *Taste of Nature*.

PART I 🌿

EDIBLE PLANTS AND RECIPES

AGAVE

Agave deserti, A. palmerii, A. perryi

Mescal, Century Plant

Features: Agaves are perennials whose prickly-edged, fleshy, blue-green leaves terminate in a needle-sharp point. Growing from a single rootstock, the uninviting young agave leaves form a rosette which can take up to 10 years to mature. Then a giant flower stalk resembling a mammoth asparagus spear appears. Stalks have been recorded as high as 40 feet, but most are much shorter, usually 9 to 15 feet tall. Although the flower stalk can grow rapidly, up to a foot a day, in the case of the century plant, it may take 30 to 40 years to bloom. In spring, the flower stalk sends out short lateral branches at the top, crowned by clusters of bright golden flowers. The flowers are replaced by firm, green, capsule-like fruits which become brown and brittle with age. Then the entire plant dries up and dies.

Facts: There are 8 species of agave throughout Arizona, New Mexico, southern Utah, southeastern California, and northern Mexico, all of which are edible when cooked. Although agaves grow throughout the year, on deserts and dry slopes, tender stalks are only available in spring for a short time before they become too tall and tough to eat. In the Southwest, young stalks and their base at the top of the root are usually gathered before they reach 3 feet in height. Raw agave is poisonous and can burn your mouth. Except for the flower petals, cooked agave is edible. Properly prepared agave is sweet and delicious. Native Americans roast the young flower stalks and their bases in rock-lined, dirt-covered pits. After uprooting the entire plant with a pointed stick, they break off most of the leaves and place the remaining stalk and base, which are about 2 feet long, in a preheated pit. Then they cover the pit with leaves and dirt, leaving the agave to roast until tender—usually overnight. Cooking time varies depending on the amount of agave roasting and the temperature of the pit. Because the roots contain saponins, they can be used for soap or shampoo when crushed and mixed with water. Mexicans make tequila from agave leaves. The leaves are very fibrous and have been used in many parts of the world to make rope. In Haiti such fibers are called *sisal*. To make it, Haitians first strip away the outer layer of the leaves, then soak the remainder and pound to release the fibers, which are then spread in the sun to dry. Finally, the fibers are rolled together to make cord.

Warning: Only the flower petals can be eaten raw; the rest of the plant is poisonous unless cooked.

FOODS

Raw: The flower petals can be eaten raw, but some taste better than others. Do not eat the entire flower or the base of the petals because they are bitter.

Cooked: Agave flower buds can be cooked before they open for a tasty vegetable similar to green beans in flavor. They can also be added to soups and stews or sautéed in butter. The root crowns and young tender flower stalks can be roasted, baked, or boiled.

BRAISED AGAVE BUDS
Serves 3–4

Water	2 tablespoons butter
1 cup firm agave buds	½ onion, chopped

Boil the buds for 10 minutes in a covered pot. Drain. Melt the butter in a frying pan and sauté the onion until clear. Stir in the buds. Cover and simmer together for 15 minutes more. Add a little water if necessary to prevent burning.

ALFALFA

Medicago sativa

Features: Alfalfa, an erect bushy perennial which grows 1 to 3 feet tall, is deeply rooting and produces 2 crops a year. Its clover-like, trifoliate leaves are comprised of 3 leaflets with slightly toothed margins, and the leaves grow alternately along stems and branches. Clusters of stunning purple flowers appear from April to October, livening up grassy slopes and fields. More mature plants sometimes become reddish near the bases of their stalks.

Facts: Because alfalfa favors moist locations, it often remains green after other plants have dried out. A native of the temperate zones of Eurasia, the Mediterranean area, and northern Africa, it is common along roads, freeways, in fields and other waste places at lower elevations. Alfalfa leaves are rich in vitamins A, K, and D, minerals, and protein, making them a nutritious addition to anyone's diet. One teaspoon of alfalfa seeds contains as much vitamin C as 10 glasses of orange juice! Native Americans in Utah ground these seeds into meal and cooked the meal with water to make a kind of mush. Ground alfalfa seed meal was also used with other kinds of meal to make bread. Alfalfa is a nitrogen-fixing herb, and its presence indicates mineral-rich soil. It also makes a good compost for poor soil. Although alfalfa is available throughout the year, most new plants appear in spring, and the best time to gather it is from late spring through early autumn.

FOODS

Tea: Put 1 teaspoon dried leaves and flowers (or 1 handful of fresh) in a mug. Add boiling water, cover, and steep for 10 minutes. The resulting tea is both mild and pleasant in flavor.

Raw: Alfalfa can be eaten raw in moderation but is somewhat difficult to digest.

Cooked: Young, tender leaves and stems can be boiled, steamed, or added to soups, stews, and stir-fries.

Seeds: Alfalfa seeds are easy to sprout, taking only 4 or 5 days to mature. The sprouts can be added to salads, sandwiches, and omelettes.

ALFALFA STIR-FRY
Serves 2

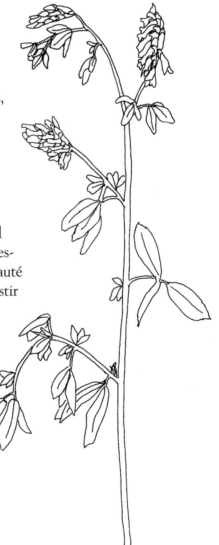

> 1 tablespoon butter
> 1 clove garlic, minced
> ½ onion, sliced
> ½ pound mushrooms,
>   sliced
> 1 cup alfalfa stems, leaves,
>   and flowers, cleaned
>   and chopped
> 1 pinch thyme
> Salt

Melt the butter in a frying pan. Sauté the garlic and onion until clear, adding more butter if necessary. Add the mushrooms and sauté until covered with butter, then stir in the alfalfa and thyme. Cover and cook over low heat until the alfalfa is wilted, adding a small amount of water if necessary to prevent burning. Season to taste with salt. Serve over rice, kasha, couscous, or baked potatoes.

BEAVERTAIL

Opuntia basilaris

Features: Beavertail is a common cactus which seldom grows over 1 foot high and has flat pads growing on top of each other. It is sometimes mistaken for the well-known prickly pear, *Opuntia littoralis*, even though prickly pear is larger and has more rounded pads. Beavertail does not have the long spines of prickly pear but has a network of glochids covering its surface. These small indentures are each filled with numerous short, brown glochid hairs, which appear soft but are painfully irritating if you come in contact with them. Beavertails range in color from whitish-green to spectacular purplish-gray, even though they are usually dull cactus green. Their rose-colored flowers bloom from March through June, and in summer the fruits appear, arranged in a line along the top of terminal pads. Smaller than prickly pear fruits, they are about the size of huge olives or small plums and turn deep rose or magenta when ripe. Flower buds and fruits can be gathered throughout the summer.

Facts: A typical desert plant, beavertail grows in dry and semiarid soil, usually below 4,000 feet. It is common in the Mojave and Colorado Deserts and sometimes grows at the bases of mountains or along coastal canyons. Not only are all parts of beavertail edible, but they have medicinal uses as well. Cahuillas used the pads to combat heart disease and diabetes. They boiled 1 pad in 3 cups of water for 5 minutes, and then drank a cup of the liquid before each meal in order to lower blood pressure. This drink was also used to treat fevers and general sickness. The pads were used by many people as a dressing for wounds. They are said to have drawing power, much like aloe vera, and they make a good Band-Aid if you are injured while hiking. The pulp can be removed from the older pads and placed directly on the wounds. To treat arthritis, the pads were steamed, peeled, and chilled, then eaten. To make a hair rinse said to decrease hair loss, some people soaked 5 pads in 1 gallon of water.

FOODS

Raw: Ripe beavertail fruits can be eaten raw, but watch out for glochids. It is easiest to harvest fruits and pads with a long-handled barbecue fork and a paper bag. Protect your working surfaces with newspaper. Peel the fruits with a knife, singe off the glochids in a fire, or dip the fruits in boiling water for several minutes and then peel them quickly before the hairs stiffen.

Cooked: Young pads can be peeled and cooked as a green bean-like vegetable, or added to scrambled eggs and salsa. The unopened flower buds are good lightly boiled or sautéed with onions. The fruits can be used to make jelly.

Dried: Beavertail pads and flower buds can be dried and stored for future use, then boiled in salted water and eaten.

Seeds: The seeds can be ground, mixed with water, and cooked into mush. This is a good way to use the seeds, which are typically discarded when you make cactus fruit jelly.

YOUNG NOPALES WITH ONIONS
Serves 2

> 3 small, young beavertail pads
> ½ cup water   1 onion, chopped
> 1 tablespoon butter   Salt and cayenne pepper

Carefully remove the skin and glochids from the cactus pads with a knife. Cut the pads into green bean-sized pieces. Put them in a pot with water and boil for 5 to 10 minutes. Taste. If the cactus is bitter, change the water and boil again. Then melt the butter in a frying pan. Sauté the onion until clear, and add the drained *nopales*. Season to taste with salt and pepper.

BUSH MALLOW

Malva fasciculatus

Features: There are many different species of *Malva*. All are edible, but some taste better than others. Highways in Arizona are brightened by the peach-colored blossoms of apricot mallow, *Sphaeralcea coulteri*. Bush mallow, which is a larger shrub growing 3 to 15 feet tall, has pale pink flowers. Marsh mallow, *Althea officinalis*, is the tallest of all the mallows, and its flowers are a lovely dusty rose. Bush mallow is either an annual or biennial bush with numerous coarse, gray-green, 3- to 5-lobed leaves growing along its slender branches. Generally blooming from April to October, fragile pink or rose-colored bush mallow flowers are made up of 5 overlapping petals and appear more bud-like than fully open. They grow alternately along the branches towards their tips and are usually not accompanied by leaves.

Facts: *Malva* is a large family which includes cotton, hibiscus, hollyhock, and okra. Its members can be used for food and medicine. In southern California, bush mallow is very common, growing in chaparral and dry waste places. The Chinese ate the leaves raw in salad or boiled as greens. Spanish-Americans boiled the leaves to make a wash. Some people used the liquid which remained after cooking as a treatment for dandruff. It was applied to freshly washed hair and then rinsed off. The roots of all species are edible. Roots that were originally used to make sore throat medicine came from marsh mallow, *Althea officinalis*. Later, this sweetened remedy was sold as a confection, and is the basis for our contemporary marshmallows. Liquid from boiled roots or leaves can be whipped into a stiff froth that can be used as a substitute for egg whites by people who cannot eat eggs. Because of their abundance and hardiness, mallows have been a welcome survival food in times of famine and were greatly valued in Rome and China.

Warning: Eat bush mallow leaves in moderation since excessive amounts have caused digestive disorders in some people.

FOODS

Raw: The young leaves of spring and early summer can be eaten raw, but they have a gritty texture and do not taste very good.

Cooked: Mallow leaves and young stems can be boiled—in several changes of water if necessary to remove bitterness. Because they tend to be mucilaginous, both the leaves and roots can be used as thickeners for soups, stews, and other dishes. The roots can be eaten as a vegetable, but usually require several changes of water to eliminate their sliminess. They can be boiled, dried off, then sautéed with onions. Mallow roots can be gathered anytime, but probably contain more nutrients if gathered before the plants bloom. Late summer is often a good time to collect the roots.

MALLOW QUICHE

Serves 4–6

Crust:
- 1 cup flour
- 4 tablespoons butter
- 2–4 tablespoons ice water

Combine the ingredients and roll out the crust. Put it in a glass pie pan and heat for 15 minutes at 375 degrees.

Filling:

1½ cups cooked bush mallow greens	
1½ cups mozzarella cheese, grated	
½ cup cottage cheese	1 clove garlic, minced
1 tablespoon olive oil	½ cup milk
1 tablespoon basil, dried	4 eggs
¼ teaspoon cayenne pepper	Parmesan cheese (optional)

Mix all the ingredients together and pour into the crust. Bake at 375 degrees for 35 to 40 minutes or until done. Remove from the oven and cool for 10 minutes before serving.

BUSHRUE

Cneoridium dumosum

Berryrue

Features: A medium-sized woody shrub, bushrue grows up to 6 feet tall and tends to spread outward. Its many branches are covered with grayish-blue bark and copious quantities of green leaves growing opposite each other in small clusters. New growth is more colorful, ranging from deep gold to dark red. From a distance, small, oblong bushrue leaves resemble rosemary leaves, but on closer inspection they are softer and more variable in size. Nestled among scrub oak, manzanita, and other common chaparral plants, bushrue usually goes unnoticed until its pristine white flowers appear. Tiny white 4-petaled bushrue flowers appear in spring, growing in small clusters along the branches and at their tips. They are later replaced by pea-sized drupes, or berries, which are almost as large as the flowers. All parts of this bush have a pleasant spicy aroma. Bushrue is often confused with spicebush, *Lindera benzoin*, since both bushes are about the same size, both grow in similar habitats, are aromatic, and produce tiny red berries. However, there are several clear differences. The most obvious difference is the flowers. Bushrue has white, 4-petaled flowers, while spicebush, or wild allspice, has yellow, 6-petaled flowers. Moreover, Spicebush can grow taller than bushrue, reaching

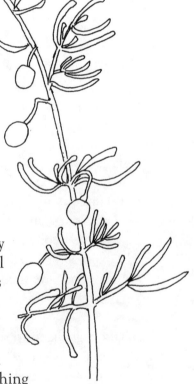

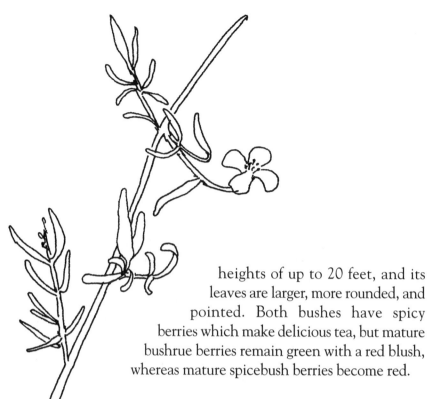

heights of up to 20 feet, and its leaves are larger, more rounded, and pointed. Both bushes have spicy berries which make delicious tea, but mature bushrue berries remain green with a red blush, whereas mature spicebush berries become red.

Facts: Bushrue grows in chaparral communities throughout the Southwest and is also found in Australia, Africa, and South America. Because bushrue blooms in spring, this is my favorite season to gather it because I can include its lovely, white flowers in my tea; however, the berries which follow have a stronger flavor.

FOODS

Tea: Put a few crushed berries and/or leaves and flowers in a cup, add boiling water, cover, and steep for 5 to 10 minutes. Strain, sweeten, and serve. For a stronger flavor, boil the berries and/or leaves with the water for 5 minutes.

CALIFORNIA BAY TREE

Umbellularia californica

Sweet Bay Laurel, California Laurel,
Oregon-Myrtle, Pepperwood

Features: Reaching heights of 20 to 50 feet, California bay trees are impressive and provide much-needed shade. In wetter climates, they may grow up to 100 feet high. Narrow, evergreen bay leaves grow 3 to 5 inches long, have smooth margins, and pointed tips. These stiff, highly aromatic leaves are dull green in color, and paler underneath than above, almost as if they were dusted with white. In spring, umbels of small, creamy-white or yellowish flowers appear. The solitary drupes which follow are about the size of small plums. Sometimes called peppernuts, they are initially dull yellow-green but become a rich purplish-brown when mature.

Facts: California bay trees grow in canyons and valleys below 5,000 feet, from California to as far north as Oregon. Because they are large trees, they require an environment that provides sufficient water. There are many uses for aromatic bay leaves. For headaches, part of a leaf was placed in the nose, or several leaves were pressed to the forehead. However, prolonged use produced new headaches. Because of their strong odor, crushed bay leaves have been used as smelling salts. Early settlers used bay leaf tea to relieve both headaches and stomachaches. For rheumatism, sufferers took a bay leaf bath. To clear the skin, a facial steam was made from chamomile, rosemary, rose petals, and bay leaves. Dried, powdered bay fruits were sometimes sprinkled over food to lower a patient's fever or increase his appetite. An oil made from the crushed leaves and berries was applied externally to provide relief from earaches, toothaches, bruises, and sprains. Greeks and Romans regarded this versatile tree so highly they honored their sports champions with crowns made from laurel leaves. Dog collars made from bay leaves, or oil from bay fruit, help repel fleas. Even if you don't have fleas, you can still hang bay branches in your home and enjoy their aroma. The best time to gather bay leaves is from April to late summer; peppernuts can be collected in summer.

FOODS

Tea: Put ½ of a small leaf in a 12-ounce mug. Add boiling water and steep for 5 minutes or less. Remove the leaf and drink when cooled. Properly prepared bay leaf tea has a pleasant flavor and a wonderful aroma.

Cooked: California bay leaves can be used in any recipe calling for bay leaves, but the amount used should be reduced because they are stronger than the ones sold in stores. They are excellent added to soups, stews, chilies, and casseroles. The French use bay

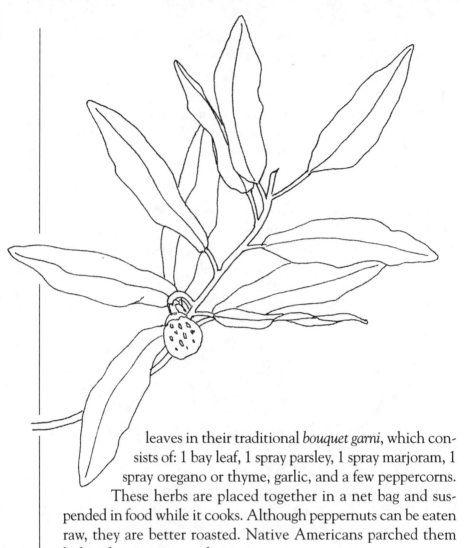

leaves in their traditional *bouquet garni*, which con-
sists of: 1 bay leaf, 1 spray parsley, 1 spray marjoram, 1
spray oregano or thyme, garlic, and a few peppercorns.
These herbs are placed together in a net bag and suspended in food while it cooks. Although peppernuts can be eaten
raw, they are better roasted. Native Americans parched them
before they were roasted.

Dried: It is best to gather bay leaves from April to late summer,
then dry them in a paper bag or other suitable container in a dark,
dry place. Peppernuts can be dried, ground, and made into bread
or cake.

HUNGARIAN GOULASH
Serves 4–6

1 tablespoon butter	2 cups tomatoes, diced
4 onions, sliced	½ bay leaf
3 cloves garlic, minced	1 teaspoon sweet paprika
1 cup flour	Salt and cayenne pepper
2½ pounds pot roast,	to taste
cubed	6 potatoes, cubed
3 tablespoons butter	

Melt 1 tablespoon butter and sauté the onions and garlic until clear. Remove from the pan and set aside. Put the flour in a large plastic bag. Add ⅓ of the meat and shake until dusted. Remove the meat and repeat this process twice until all of the meat is dusted with flour. Melt 1 tablespoon of butter in a frying pan and brown ⅓ of the meat. Remove the meat and repeat this procedure twice, melting 1 tablespoon of butter and browning ⅓ of the dusted meat until all the meat is browned. Clean the pan between cookings if necessary. Then put the meat and onions in a large pot. Add the tomatoes and seasonings. Cover and cook slowly for 1 hour. Stir occasionally, adding a little water if necessary to prevent sticking. Add the potatoes and continue cooking for another hour.

CALIFORNIA FAN PALM

Washingtonia filifera

Features: The California fan palm has a tall, gray, unbranched, sometimes gently arched trunk which can grow up to 75 feet tall and up to 40 inches in diameter. It is crowned with a cluster of large, graceful, fan-shaped leaves which are 5 to 6 feet long and have spiny margins. New green leaves, which grow almost vertically from the center of the top of the trunk, fade in color and droop as they age. Older leaves hang down along the sides of the trunk, providing needed shade, shelter for birds and rodents, and help the tree retain moisture. California fan palms bloom in June, and in summer up to 10 large clusters of date berries, or drupes, weighing from 5 to 20 pounds each, hang from each tree. In a good year one tree may produce up to 12 clusters. Each date is about the size of a small grape and contains a single, large seed.

Facts: California's only native palm, *Washingtonia filifera* is a good indicator of the presence of water, and can be found growing in sandy or rocky washes and open alkaline soil near springs and streams from Death Valley, south to Mexico, and east to southern Nevada and western Arizona. These palms were more than a source of food for Native Americans. The large, convenient leaves were often used for roofing. Fiber obtained from these palm fronds was made into skirts, baskets, cord, and sandals. Seeds from the dates were used to make rattles, or saved, dried, ground, and made into flour, which was used for gruel or bread. The fruit was gathered from late summer through early autumn, and was eaten fresh or dried. Sometimes the dried fruits were soaked in water to produce a mild-flavored beverage.

FOODS

Tea: A mild tea can be made from the water in which the dates are soaked.

Raw: The dates are small and contain large seeds, and their thin, sweet, edible pulp is delicious.

Cooked: The dates can be made into jelly. The heart of the palm is edible and very tasty. However, it should only be eaten in emergencies since the tree has to be destroyed in order to acquire the heart, which is located in the center of the trunk. Fan palm leaf bases can also be eaten.

Dried: The date seeds can be dried and ground into a sweet-flavored meal. The dates can be dried in the sun and stored for future use.

CALIFORNIA WALNUT

Juglans californica

Features: Native California walnut trees are small trees or large shrubs, which under optimal conditions grow as tall as 30 feet. With their broad, bushy crowns, they provide welcome shade. The leaves are compound, with 4 to 7 pairs of leaflets and 1 or occasionally 2 terminal leaflets. Each dark green leaflet is slender and minutely toothed. New bark is silvery-brown, becoming rougher and darker with age. California walnuts are smaller than English walnuts—closer to the size of black walnuts. Over summer and fall they grow singly, in pairs, or in small clusters at the tips of the branches, surrounded by a halo of leaves radiating outward like the rays of the sun. Each nut is covered by a hard shell which is encased in a pulpy husk.

Facts: California walnut trees grow along streams and washes located in warm parts of California, Arizona, New Mexico, and northern Mexico. They prefer higher elevations, usually altitudes between 3,500 and 7,000 feet. Be careful when handling the husks encasing the walnuts. Not only do they stain your hands and clothes, but they smell bad, somewhat like an unpleasant blend of old bandages and antiseptic. Some Native Americans buried the walnuts for several days until the husks rotted away. The shells of California walnuts are harder than those of the English walnuts in stores. The easiest way to crack them is with a hammer, placing clean newspaper under them first. In Canada, some Native American braves put several walnuts in each moccasin and ran until the nuts were cracked open. However, this is not recommended for the average "tenderfoot." Native Americans also brewed a tea from the leaves to use as a blood purifier and stomach aid. According to some sources, walnuts help reduce cholesterol. The nuts, which begin to appear in spring, are usually ready to harvest by late summer or early fall. Wait until they reach their full size, and then put them in the sun until the husks begin to dry out and turn brown.

FOODS

Raw: Walnuts are delicious raw as a snack or added to salads, cereals, trail mix, stir-fries, and Jell-O molds. After the nuts are husked, it is best to let them dry out for a week or two before shelling and eating them.

WALDORF SALAD
Serves 4–6

4 apples, peeled and diced	½ cup raisins
4 stalks celery, sliced	½ cup mayonnaise
½ cup walnuts, chopped	2 carrots, grated
Juice from 2 oranges	

Mix all the ingredients and serve.

WALNUT LOAF
Serves 2–4

2 cups carrots, grated	Salt and cayenne pepper
1½ cups cheddar cheese, grated	4 eggs, beaten
1 medium onion, grated	1 cup walnuts, chopped
½ cup parsley or	½ cup milk
2 tablespoons cilantro, chopped	½ cup flour
	1 cup cooked rice (optional)

Mix the ingredients together and bake in a greased glass baking dish at 375 degrees until done, about 1 hour. Insert a knife; if it comes out clean, the loaf is done. The deeper the pan used, the more time required to cook the loaf.

CANAIGRE

Rumex hymenosepalus

Dock, Wild Rhubarb, Red Dock, Pie Plant

Features: Canaigre is a large, hardy perennial herb which generally grows from 2 to 4 feet high. It is native to the Southwest, and there are 20 species of dock growing in New Mexico alone. Canaigre is an early spring plant and under favorable conditions may appear as early as February. Most of canaigre's leaves are basal. Thick and green, with smooth, curled margins, these large, narrow leaves grow 6 to 18 inches long and up to 2 inches in diameter. Their surfaces are also smooth. A single, slightly branched flower stalk rises stiffly from their centers. Tiny greenish flowers go unnoticed, replaced by decorative triangular seeds suspended in bunches, and arranged in tiers like miniature paper lanterns. Green at first, in summer and fall they become warm reddish-brown. Canaigre is often confused with curly dock, *Rumex crispus*, which is not a major problem since both plants are edible. Their leaves and seeds are very similar, but their structure differs. Almost all of canaigre's large leaves meet at ground level, while curly dock's leaves grow along its stalk and branches. Canaigre's leaves and seeds are larger, but its flower stalk is shorter. Curly dock has more branches and more seeds. Both grow from a stout rootstock which contains tannin and can be used to tan leather; however, canaigre roots contain more tannin, up to 35 percent.

Facts: Canaigre grows throughout the West, along sandy streambeds and in fields at elevations below 5,000 feet. Native Americans of New Mexico ate the young stems and leaves raw, or roasted and saved them for winter to mix with beans. They also ground the seeds, mixed them with water, and formed flat cakes or cooked mush. Canaigre leaves contain significant amounts of vitamins A and C. Oxalic acid is also present and provides a refreshing lemony flavor. Although cooking is said to neutralize this acid, it is always wise to eat foods containing oxalic acid—

such as rhubarb, cranberries, spinach, sour grass, curly dock, and canaigre—in moderation. Because of their similarity, young canaigre stems can be used as a substitute in recipes calling for rhubarb. Canaigre's roots contain leucodelphin and leucopelargonidan, two chemicals used in chemotherapy.

Warning: Canaigre leaves contain oxalic acid, excessive amounts of which can be harmful. Use leaves in moderation.

FOODS
Raw: Young, tender leaves, which are usually available from February through summer and again in fall, make a tasty addition to salads and sandwiches but should be eaten in moderation.

Cooked: Crisp canaigre leaves are best used in combination with other, milder greens because of their strong but pleasant lemony flavor. They are especially suited to stir-fries because they do not cook down as much as other leaves. If the leaves are older and somewhat bitter, they can be cooked in 2 changes of water. Canaigre leaves and stems taste best boiled or roasted.

Dried: Canaigre leaves can be dried by roasting or other methods, and saved for winter.

CANAIGRE SAUCE
Serves 2
> 2 cups tender stalks,
>   cut in ½-inch pieces
> ½ cup sugar
> 1 cup water

Mix all the ingredients together and place them in a pot, cover, and bring to a boil. Lower the heat and simmer for 5 to 10 minutes, then cool. This tangy dish can be served as a dessert or relish. It also makes a good ice cream or yogurt topping which is not only tasty but attractive as well.

CAROB

Ceratonia siliqua

St. John's Bread, Locust Bread, Locust Tree, Monkey Bread

Features: Drought-resistant, evergreen carob is considered a small tree, although it generally grows from 20 to 40 feet high, and its many spreading branches create a dense crown. These branches are covered with compound leaves made up of 3 to 5 pairs of shiny, leathery, oval leaflets which grow about 1½ inches long and are sometimes notched at the tip. Each leaflet has a tiny, individual stem. In spring, racemes of small, dull, greenish-brown, petalless flowers are hardly noticeable. This is not true of the clusters of long, leathery seedpods which follow. Growing in small clusters, these large seedpods measure 4 to 10 inches long and 1 to 1½ inches wide. Pale green and somewhat tender initially, they rapidly become brown and brittle as they mature. Inside their hard exterior is a tender, edible, smelly lining and several indestructible pinto bean-sized seeds.

Facts: Carob is a native to the eastern Mediterranean region and extensively planted throughout southern California. Carob pods are rich in protein and sugar, containing up to 50 percent sugar when dried. They are used as food as well as cattle feed. Because carob pods are also known as "locusts," many scholars believe that they are the food referred to in the Bible as John the Baptist's wilderness diet of "locusts and honey." Carob is a good sweetener, an excellent caffeine-free coffee or chocolate substitute, an ice cream thickener, and an aid in the assimilation of other foods. Moreover, carob seeds were once used as a standard of weight. In East Germany near Breslau, imported carob pods were sold in the markets like candy. Children would buy several pods and eat them, spitting out the seeds. I met one of these children, now a charming, white-haired adult, at Quail Gardens in Encinitas, California. We sampled the local mature carob pods. Although they were prime—large and brown but not yet brittle—they were not as tasty as the ones she remembered.

FOODS

Tea/Hot Drink: For 3 cups of carob drink, clean 2 carob pods and break them into pieces. Boil them with 2½ cups of water in a covered pot for 15 minutes. Remove the pods and add ½ cup milk. For cocoa: Mix 1 part sugar with 3 parts of carob powder. Use like regular cocoa with hot milk.

Raw: The entire pod can be eaten. Just spit out the seeds. They taste a lot better than they smell.

Cooked: There are many delicious recipes which call for carob powder. Pick the pods after they turn brown but before they become brittle. Clean them and remove the seeds. For cooking, the entire pod, with the seeds removed, can be ground into powder in a hand mill or flour mill, or the soft lining of the pods can be scraped off. Most pods are mature by September or October.

GIANT CAROB COOKIE
Makes 1 10-inch cookie

1 egg	½ cup flour
¼ cup sugar	⅛ teaspoon baking powder
½ teaspoon vanilla	⅛ teaspoon salt
3 tablespoons butter	¼ cup walnuts, chopped
¼ cup carob pod lining, chopped, or carob powder	

Mix the egg, sugar, and vanilla together. Melt the butter and add the carob. Heat together for 1 to 2 minutes. Then combine all the ingredients in a bowl. Grease a 10-inch glass pie pan. Pour the batter into the pan and bake at 350 degrees for 20 minutes or until done.

CHECKERBLOOM

Sidalcea malvaeflora

Features: Perennial checkerbloom is always an unexpected treat when discovered growing hidden among the taller grasses of meadows and streambeds. Although checkerbloom grows from 8 inches to 2 feet tall, it is usually under 1 foot in height. The plants often go unnoticed since they hang over the ground. They have 2 distinctive sets of leaves. Small clusters of heart-shaped slightly fuzzy leaves with scalloped margins announce the arrival of plants. Then a slender, stiff, slightly hairy flower stalk arises from the midst of these basal leaves with smaller, palmate, 5-lobed leaves growing along its length. Later, delicate, 5-petaled, pale pink mallow-like flowers grow alternately near the top of the stalk, clustering at its tip. Before their distinctive flowers appear, young checkerbloom plants can be mistaken for immature larkspur plants, *Delphinium* spp., which grow in the same environment and are poisonous. However, once they bloom in spring, the differences are obvious. Not only is larkspur a taller, sturdier plant, but the bright blue or red spurred flowers grow up the flower stalk, whereas checkerbloom's pale, fragile, 5-petaled flowers grow mostly near the top of their much shorter flower stalk.

Facts: Fragile checkerbloom plants grow throughout the West in alkali soil. Even though checkerbloom's leaves are edible, it is not advisable to pick them until after the flowers appear to avoid confusing checkerbloom with larkspur.

FOODS
Tea: Put 6 fresh leaves or 1 tablespoon dried leaves in a cup, add boiling water, cover, and steep for 5 minutes. Do not oversteep because the tea will become bitter. Properly prepared tea is both mild and pleasant.

Raw: The young leaves and stems of spring and summer can be eaten raw, but be sure that you have checkerbloom and not larkspur.

Cooked: Fuzzy checkerbloom leaves can be cooked, but they are not very interesting and are best when added to more flavorful leaves or used in soups or stews.

EGG DROP SOUP

Serves 3–4

> 1 quart chicken broth (preferably homemade)
> ¼ cup checkerbloom leaves, cleaned and chopped
> 1 teaspoon sweet paprika
> 4 eggs
> Salt and
>   cayenne pepper

Bring the broth to a boil. Stir in the leaves. Cover and keep at a low boil for 2 to 3 minutes. Add the paprika and eggs, stirring the eggs constantly with a fork. (If the eggs are not stirred, they will form lumps, and if the liquid is not boiling, you will have a murky liquid instead of streamers of cooked egg.) Cook for 2 to 3 minutes more, until the eggs are ready. Season to taste with salt and pepper.

CHICORY

Cichorium intybus

Blue Sailors, Succory, Chicory Lettuce, Wild Endive

Features: A wand-like perennial growing from 1 to 4 feet high, chicory is easy to spot, especially after its beautiful blue flowers appear. A hardy plant that makes its debut with a basal cluster of long, toothed leaves, chicory soon produces several upright stalks from a single, stout taproot. As the stalks grow, they begin to branch slightly. Both stalks and branches are sparsely adorned with stemless leaves which are smaller in size than the original basal ones. Although the new growth is smooth, flexible, and green, it becomes rough and reddish with age, and the older stalks are gritty near their bases. Underneath the leaves are pronounced spines which have short white hairs. Chicory flowers grow in the leaf joints, alternately along the top

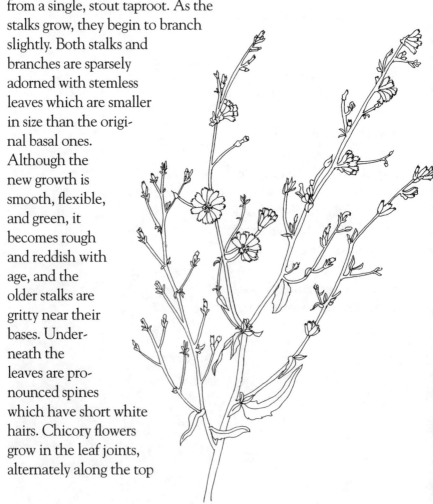

portion of stalks and branches, usually unaccompanied by leaves. Although their many fringed petals are sometimes pale blue or white, most often they are bright blue. The flowers on a single plant do not all bloom at the same time. And it is said that some varieties of chicory only bloom at noon on sunny days, whereas other varieties bloom throughout the day. People sometimes mistake basal chicory leaves for dandelion leaves. Both have a ragged appearance, although chicory leaves are longer and their lobes shallower. Also, underneath their leaves the spines have short white hairs.

Facts: Originally from Europe, chicory grows in untended yards, waste places, fields, and along roadsides throughout the world. Chicory leaves are high in vitamin A and reputedly beneficial to the liver and gallbladder. The root is considered a good liver tonic. Poultices can be made from the leaves and used to soothe inflammations. With a little effort chicory leaves can be made available year-round. If the roots are planted in a container of soil and placed in a cellar or other dark location, a cluster of white (blanched) leaves will grow. The French call these forced leaves *barb du capucin capuchin*, while others call them "chicons." Italians call chicory *radicchio*. Chicory usually blooms from late spring through early autumn. Pick young, tender leaves from late March to early July for salads, since older leaves are too bitter.

FOODS
Tea: A mild tea can be brewed from the fresh leaves. Put 1 tablespoon of dried or 2 tablespoons of fresh clean leaves in a mug, add boiling water, cover, and let steep for 10 minutes. Strain and serve.

Raw: Use the leaves as you would dandelion leaves, remembering that they tend to be bitter, and are best when added to other, milder greens. It is always preferable to pick leaves before flower stalks appear. Some people like to dip the young leaves for 1 minute in boiling water before eating them. Chicory leaves can be made into

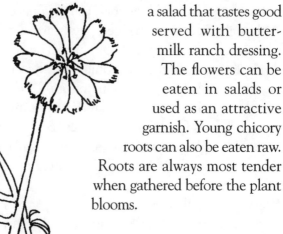

a salad that tastes good served with butter-milk ranch dressing. The flowers can be eaten in salads or used as an attractive garnish. Young chicory roots can also be eaten raw. Roots are always most tender when gathered before the plant blooms.

Cooked: The leaves can be cooked like spinach but may require more than 1 change of water if they are bitter. The young roots can be boiled or roasted, and taste good served with a cream sauce, but they are best known as a coffee substitute or extender. Although people have contradictory opinions about the best time to gather chicory roots for the purpose of preparing a hot, coffee-like beverage, most favor late summer.

CHICORY SALAD
Makes 5 cups

2 cups lettuce	1 tablespoon green onions
1 cup young chicory leaves	2 tomatoes, chopped

Mix and serve with Italian dressing.

ITALIAN DRESSING
Makes ¼ cup

2 cloves garlic, minced	½ teaspoon salt
1 tablespoon vinegar	Cayenne pepper to taste
3 tablespoons olive oil	

Blend the ingredients together.

HOT CHICORY "COFFEE"
Chicory roots
Water

Scrub the roots well and slice them length-wise. Brown them slowly in a low oven until they are brown all the way through, or slice them into thin strips and dry them in the sun for 24 hours. Next roast them in the oven at a low temperature about 1 hour, or until they are golden brown. Then grind the brown, brittle roots in a coffee grinder or blender. Brew them as you would coffee or add them to coffee, substituting ½ tea-spoon of ground chicory for 1 tablespoon of ground coffee when brewing a 6-cup pot. Coffee drink-ers tell me that this hot chicory drink does not really taste like coffee, but some actually prefer it.

CRAB APPLE

Malus spp.

Features: The crab apple tree is said to be parent to our domestic apple tree, *Malus domestica*. There are 35 species of crab apple tree, most of which tend to be small, only growing from 6 to 12 feet tall. They have many branches, which are covered with numerous ovate leaves growing on short stems. From late April until early June, clusters of lovely, fragile, 5-petaled white flowers shaded with pale pink appear. Following these sweet-scented flowers are hanging bunches of miniature cherry-sized apples, which become dusty-red when ripe, from September through November.

Facts: Crab apple trees grow in the sunny, well-drained soil of open woodlands and do best with a bit of cold weather. They can be found in northern Europe, Asia, and scattered throughout the north temperate zone. The apples are incredibly healthful. Not only are they full of minerals and vitamins, especially A and C, they also contain significant amounts of calcium, pectin, and a predigested form of sugar. They help in the absorption of iron from other foods, are a good blood purifier, and benefit the lymphatic system. People who say "eat an apple a day" know what they are talking about. Since the time of ancient Egypt, apples have been used for both food and medicine—to relieve gout, soothe bilious conditions, and calm nerves. They were combined with saffron to form a mixture that was eaten for relief from jaundice. Apples were even rubbed on warts in the hope of removing them. Today, doctors prescribe grated apples in stubborn cases of diarrhea, especially for babies since it is gentle and not harmful. However, apple seeds contain cyanide and can be deadly when eaten in excess. There is a well-known legend about a man who used to save his apple seeds in a jar. One night while he was watching television, he got the "munchies." Rather than go to the kitchen for a snack, he reached for his apple seed jar and during the course of the evening devoured all the seeds. The following morning his neighbor found his dead body slumped in front of the television.

Warning: Do not eat apple seeds, especially in quantity. They contain cyanide and can kill you. Also avoid eating the flowers, which may contain cyanide precursors.

FOODS

Tea: Put some apple peels in a mug, fill with boiling water, cover, and steep for 5 to 10 minutes. Apple peel tea is mild-flavored, sweetly scented, and said to be good for the kidneys.

Raw: Crab apples are juicy and can be eaten raw, but they are very sour unless sweetened.

Cooked: Cooked crab apples make delicious breads, cakes, pies, jellies, jams, chutneys, and drinks. When you cook any apples, try to keep the temperature low, because heat destroys vitamins and minerals.

CRAB APPLE BUTTER
Makes about 1 pint

2 cups crab apples, cleaned and halved	¾ teaspoon cinnamon
	1 cup sugar
¼ cup water	¼ teaspoon ginger and/
6 tablespoons lemon juice	or cloves

Heat the crab apples, water, and lemon juice together. Bring to a boil, then lower the heat. Cover and simmer, stirring occasionally, until the apples are soft and sauce-like. Add the sugar and spices and stir until well blended. Remove from the stove; dish into a container. This delicious sauce may be served hot or cold.

DAY LILY

Hemerocallis spp.

Features: Lovely, colorful, perennial, herbaceous day lilies originally came from Japan. These prolific plants spread by rhizomes.
Several slender, slightly branched flower stalks rise stiffly from a
sea of 5 to 8 leathery, grass-like leaves. Each flower stalk, usually
growing from 2 to 3 feet tall, bears 6 to 8 flowers and no leaves. As
their name implies, each flower blooms for only one day. But,
because they do not all bloom at the same time, they appear to last
much longer. Although there are hybrid colors, most day lilies are
either sunny yellow (*Hemerocallis fulva*) or bright golden-orange
(*H. flava*). Day lily roots are large and fibrous with clusters of small,
elongated, edible tubers growing directly below.

Facts: May to September are the best times for spotting these fun-
nel-shaped blossoms. Since they are a popular decorative plant,
they can be found growing almost anywhere. Naturalized day lily
plants favor the well-drained soil of waste places, open areas, and
roadsides. If you want to collect some of the tubers but cause as
little damage as possible, wait until April to November. Dig up
the entire plant, remove only some of the tubers, then replant it.
Both fresh and dried, day lily buds are very popular in the Orient.
The Chinese and the Japanese especially like to eat them combined with pork and soy sauce. All parts of all varieties of day
lilies are edible unless they have been exposed to pesticides or
other chemicals.

Warning: Because day lilies have diuretic properties, eat them in moderation.

FOODS
Raw: The flowers, flower buds, shoots, and small, firm tubers can
all be eaten raw. The young shoots are best gathered in April.

Cooked: The flower buds are delicious cooked—even better than
the green beans to which they are often compared. Pick them just

before they open, then boil, steam, or stir-fry them. They can also be added to soups and stews, or dipped in batter and fried. Young stalks can be cooked like asparagus. Opened flowers taste good in pancakes and omelettes, and even withered flowers can be added to soups and stews. Tender young tubers can be cleaned, then boiled or steamed until tender.

Dried: The flowers and buds are easy to dry and store for future use. Soak them in cold water until soft before cooking.

DAY LILY-BLUEBERRY PANCAKES
Based on a recipe from *Edible Flowers from Garden to Palate* by Cathy Wilkinson Barash.
Serves 2

4 eggs	2 tablespoons sugar
1 cup cottage cheese	½ teaspoon vanilla
1 pinch salt	1 cup fresh blueberries
2 tablespoons	Petals from 5 day lilies,
butter, melted	chopped
½ cup flour	Oil

Blend the first 7 ingredients together. Gently fold in the berries and petals. A light touch now will produce light pancakes. Heat oil on a griddle or in a frying pan and cook the pancakes.

STEAMED DAY LILY BUDS
Water
Day lily buds, cleaned
Butter
Salt

Boil a little water. Add the day lily buds, cover, and steam for 5 minutes. Drain and serve with butter and salt.

DUDLEYA

Dudleya pulverulenta

Chalk Dudleya, Chalk Lettuce,
Chalk Live-Forever, Deer's Tongue

Features: Many different succulent plants belong to the Dudleya family. Chalk dudleya is a perennial which grows quite large; it is usually the size of a healthy head of lettuce but can be as large as 18 inches across. Its layered leaves are rectangular, coming to a point at their terminal ends. Although they are actually grayish-blue in color, these thick, succulent leaves appear much lighter because they are dusted with a white bloom which comes off on your hands. In spring, chalk dudleya sends up several flower stalks which grow up to 16 inches high. Small clusters of tiny, pale red flowers grow along the flower stalks and at their tips. The flowers and flower stalks are also covered with white, powdery bloom. These unusual plants are hard to miss, especially after chalk lettuce flower stalks turn red. By the time the flower stalks are mature, the "lettuce" leaves have begun to dry up and wither away. Tiny, scale-like leaves grow along the flower stalks, and they remain while the flowers blossom. A related dudleya called lady's fingers, or mission lettuce (*Dudleya edulis*), is a fairly common dudleya in southern California. The young

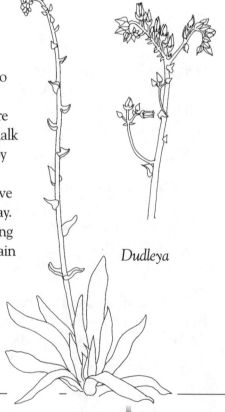

Dudleya

plants consist of a cluster of cylindrical, basal leaves, each of which resembles a skinny, jointless, elongated lady's finger. This plant also has a flower stalk.

Facts: Chalk live-forever is common in southern California, and can be found growing on rocky slopes which face south or west at elevations below 2,000 feet. They say that "beauty is in the eye of the beholder," and perhaps this is true of taste as well. Although Cahuillas and other Native Americans not only ate the different dudleyas but actually enjoyed them, no matter how many times I have sampled chalk lettuce and lady's fingers, they do not taste good and always leave a bitter taste in my mouth. Since many species are on the rare and endangered list, it is probably just as well that they are not very popular. Chalk lettuce leaves were used to remove corns and calluses. A large leaf was heated over a fire and its skin peeled off one side. Then the warm leaf was put on the offending corn or callus and left there overnight. Moreover, tea made from boiled chalk lettuce leaves was used as a cure for asthma. As is true of most plants, the best time to gather the leaves is when they are young, before the flower stalks appear in spring. Look for dudleya hidden among the rocks along cliffs and canyons.

FOODS
Raw: The leaves and flower stems can be eaten raw, although they do not taste good to most people.

Lady's Fingers

FIREWEED

Epilobium angustifolium

Great Willow Herb, Rose Bay

Features: Stately, perennial fireweed has a single, unbranched stalk which grows from 1½ to 8 feet tall. Long, narrow, willow-like fireweed leaves are dark green above and silvery underneath. This plant is hard to miss, especially when in bloom from July to September. Four-petaled, fuchsia-colored flowers, each on a short flower stem, form a pyramid shape towards the top of the plant. Because fireweed usually grows in a large community connected by creeping rootstocks, when it is in bloom, the whole area looks like a sea of color. After blooming, the flowers fall off, but the show is not over yet. Entire plants then become brilliant fiery red, and long, narrow seedpods form, later releasing feathery seeds which float away or cover the ground.

Facts: There are dozens of species of fireweed found throughout the West, growing in moist, rich soil as well as in burned-out or cut-over areas. It usually grows at higher elevations up to 9,000 feet. Fireweed does well with a little cold weather and can be found growing as far north as Alaska. These plants are high in vitamins A and C. In Europe the young spring fireweed shoots are cooked like asparagus and eaten. They have also been used medicinally to promote the healing of sores and to help boils and cuts drain. A mildly laxative tea made from fireweed leaves is used as a spring tonic or to settle upset stomachs. Native Americans even found a purpose for the fluffy seeds, which they used as a wool substitute, mixing them with mountain goat wool or duck feathers.

FOODS
Tea: Put 4 to 6 fresh leaves or 1 teaspoon dried leaves in a mug. Add boiling water, cover, and steep for 5 minutes. Remove the leaves and serve. Fireweed tea has a mild, pleasant flavor.

Raw: The pith, the white inner portion of young stems, is sweet and can be eaten raw. The flowers, flower buds, and roots, as well as the young leaves, can also be eaten raw.

Cooked: Tender young shoots can be steamed, boiled, or stir-fried. They usually only need to be boiled for a few minutes before they are ready to eat. However, if they are still bitter, change the water and boil them again. Their flavor varies depending on the conditions under which they grew but usually is slightly spicy like a mild nasturtium leaf. Unopened buds can be cooked. The pith can be removed from older stems and used as a thickening agent in soups and stews.

FIREWEED "HONEY"
Makes 4 pints
2½ cups water
1 teaspoon alum
10 cups sugar
18 fireweed flowers
30 white clover flowers
18 red clover flowers

Boil the water, alum, and sugar together for 10 minutes, being careful not to let the mixture boil over. Remove from the heat. Add all the flowers and steep for 15 minutes. Strain out the flowers and pour the remaining liquid into 4 sterile glass jars. Close with lids and rubber seals and store in a dark location for as long as you like. Fireweed honey keeps well.

GOAT'S BEARD

Tragopogon pratensis

Yellow Goat's Beard

Features: Goat's beard is an elusive perennial herb with slender, unbranched flower stalks which grow up to 3 feet tall. Long, grass-like leaves with jagged margins grow at their bases. From spring to midsummer, lovely, yellow, daisy-like flowerheads, supported by leaf-like bracts, appear, only remaining open during the early part of the day. Usually they resemble long, tightly closed buds. This helps to explain why goat's beard plants can remain so well-hidden in the dry grassy places where they grow. However, when they go to seed, it is another matter. Huge, beautiful, spherical, dandelion-like seed-heads as large as tennis balls form, with each seed looking like an interconnected floating star.

Goat's beard, which belongs to a genus of 40 species, is often confused with salsify, *Tragopogon porrifolius*, which looks very similar. However, *T. porrifolius* has purple flowerheads and is biennial. Although *T. pratensis* is sometimes called salsify, *T. porrifolius* is never called goat's beard but is always referred to as salsify or oyster root. Even chicory, *Cichorium intybus*, is occasionally called salsify. This is surprising, because the two plants do not resemble each other, although their roots appear similar and have similar medicinal properties. Like goat's beard, salsify blooms from April to July, and its flowers remain open only during the early hours of the day.

Facts: Goat's beard grows on open ground, in dry grassy fields, and in thickets throughout the United States. Both goat's beard and salsify come from the Mediterranean region, where salsify's oyster-flavored roots were cooked and enjoyed. Juice from goat's beard and salsify is said to relieve heartburn. In Canada, Native Americans chew the latex-laden roots of goat's beard like gum.

FOODS
Raw: In spring the young leaves and flower buds can be used in salads.

Cooked: Roots, young shoots, and flower buds from both goat's beard and salsify can be pickled, boiled, or roasted. The thick, white taproots cook quickly. The top of the rootstalk, known as the crown, is also very tasty. Cut the root off 3 inches below the ground, leaving the rest to propagate. Cut off most of the stem and leaves, then cook the remaining crowns until tender. Roots are best when gathered from spring until fall.

BOILED GOAT'S BEARD
Goat's beard roots
Butter
Salt and cayenne pepper

Boil the cleaned roots until they are tender. Drain off the water. Peel, dice, and serve with butter, salt, and pepper.

GOOSEBERRY

Ribes speciosum

Fuchsia-Flowered Gooseberry

Features: Densely branched gooseberry bushes are thorny perennials which grow up to 8 feet high. In general, the thorny species which have spiny fruit are called gooseberries. The bushes without thorns, which bear smooth fruit, are called currants. Sharp, red spines grow along gooseberry branches. Gooseberry's numerous leaves have 3 lobes each and are covered with tiny white hairs. Each of the lobes is subdivided into smaller lobes. These leaves grow singly or in small bunches of different-sized leaves, alternately along the grayish-brown branches on individual stems. The branches are so numerous, and some grow so low on the trunk, that often there are branches trailing over the ground. In spring, tiny, 5-petaled, fuchsia-colored flowers hang suspended in small bunches along the branches. As they age, they dry up and wither but do not drop off. Instead, they hang like tassels from the bottoms of the developing berries. Spiny, translucent, gumball-sized gooseberries, which appear in late spring, become purplish-red or remain yellowish-green when they mature by summer, depending on their variety. Green gooseberries are attractively decorated with contrasting green watermelon-like stripes which run from top to bottom.

Facts: Gooseberry bushes grow in moist locations and shaded canyons in temperate zones throughout the world. There are about 150 species in all, with 80 species growing in North America. The berries, high in vitamin C and copper, are often recommended for convalescents as an appetite stimulant. Gooseberry bushes have been grown in European gardens since the sixteenth century and were among the vitamin C-rich plants eaten during World War I to prevent scurvy. Gooseberries are diuretic, and have been used to help dissipate fevers. Native Americans combined them with meat and fat to make a form of dried food called pemmican, which they took with them on long journeys. Eating these spiny berries right off the bush is tricky, but Native Americans are so skillful at this that they can insert a berry in their mouth, remove the skin, and swallow the rest without a problem.

FOODS

Tea: Since many leaves steeped in a mug of water only produce a very mild tea, gooseberry leaves are more often used as an addition to other tea blends than by themselves.

Raw: Juicy gooseberries are both sweet and tart when eaten raw. They can be peeled by hand if necessary.

Cooked: Because of their spines, it is often easier to cook the berries than eat them raw. They can be sweetened to taste, and made into delicious jellies, jams, pies, syrups, and chutneys. Ripe or nearly ripe berries can be used. Nearly ripe berries require no pectin when made into jelly.

Dried: The berries can be dried and cooked later or eaten as snacks.

Frozen: The berries can be frozen for later use. Wash them and remove the stem ends. Then put them in containers and freeze.

FRUIT LEATHER
Based on a recipe from *Discovering Wild Plants* by Janice J. Schofield.
>   4 cups gooseberries
>   1 cup water
>   2 cups sugar or 1 cup honey

Simmer the berries in the water until soft. Stir in the sugar or honey. Put a piece of Saran Wrap in a glass pan or on a cookie sheet. Spread the fruit mixture thinly and evenly over the surface. Heat until dry and flexible but not brittle, in a low oven or out in the sun. If you are using sunlight, you may want to put a lightweight, breathable fabric such as muslin lightly over the fruit leather to protect your treat from interested insects.

Old-Fashioned Gooseberry Tapioca Pie Filling or Pudding

Makes about 2 cups
> 2 cups almost ripe gooseberries
> 1 cup water
> 3 cups sugar
> 6 tablespoons tapioca

Combine the gooseberries and 1 cup water in a pot. Crush the berries, cover, and simmer for ½ hour. Strain. Set the liquid aside and stir in the sugar and tapioca. Wait 5 minutes for the tapioca to soften, then heat the mixture over medium heat until the mixture thickens, stirring constantly.

Crust:
> 1 cup flour
> 4 tablespoons butter
> 2–4 tablespoons ice water

Prepare the crust. Put it in a greased pie pan and heat at 375 degrees for 10 minutes, then set it aside.

HEDGE MUSTARD

Sisymbrium officinale

Flax Weed

Features: Hedge mustard is a delicate, erect annual which grows up to 21 inches tall. It is slightly branched and sparsely adorned with dull green leaves. The leaves vary in shape and size, with the largest ones being those closest to the ground. Most of the leaves are basal. Each leaf is once or twice divided and has a large terminal lobe which is shaped like a rimmed hat. Their margins are irregular. In spring, the entire plant is covered with small, soft hairs, especially near the base. Hedge mustard has yellow, 4-petaled flowers which are typical of mustard plants. However, in the case of hedge mustard, these flowers are not merely small but minute and grow in clusters at the tips of the stalks and branches. The flowers are followed by small, oval, brown seeds which grow atop the stalk and branches.

Facts: Hedge mustard grows in early spring, in a wide variety of places, including open fields, deserts, waste places, scrub, grasslands, oak woodlands, and chaparral in most states and particularly throughout the West. Its seeds, which are rich in vitamin C, were the part most used by Native Americans and Mexicans for food and medicine. These seeds, called *palmito* in Spanish, can be gathered from late summer until early fall. They are sold in drugstores to be crushed and made into poultices, or to be brewed into tea. Until the eighteenth century, this tea was considered the number-one cure for laryngitis and other throat ailments. Hedge mustard was also used to cure colds, pleurisy, sciatica, and canker sores. Native Americans gathered the seeds by knocking them into baskets. Following this, the seeds were parched, ground, and made into mush or added to soup. Pomos used them to flavor acorn meal.

FOODS

Raw: Young leaves, picked in spring before the plants flower, can be added to salads and sandwiches.

Cooked: The leaves are usually cooked as a potherb but can be added, in moderation, to omelettes, quiches, soups, and stews. If they are bitter, try cooking them in 2 changes of water. The seeds can be parched and ground into flour or cooked into mush.

HEDGE MUSTARD CASSEROLE

Serves 2–4

> 1 cup hedge mustard leaves, cleaned and chopped
> 1 tablespoon butter
> 3 tablespoons flour
> 1 cup milk
> ½ cup cheddar cheese, grated
> Salt and cayenne pepper
> 2 eggs, beaten
> 3 cups lamb's quarters leaves,
>   cleaned and chopped
> 3 tablespoons Parmesan cheese

Steam the greens in a small quantity of water until wilted. Separate the cooked greens and their liquid, retaining both. Meanwhile, prepare a cheese sauce. Melt the butter. Slowly add the flour and stir until blended. A little at a time, add the milk and up to ½ cup of retained cooking liquid. Turn down the heat. When the sauce is smoothly blended, add the cheddar cheese and season to taste with salt and pepper. Remove from the stove and combine with the eggs and the cooked greens. Pour into a greased baking pan, sprinkle with the Parmesan cheese, and bake at 325 degrees for about 20 minutes or until firm. Serve hot.

HEDGE NETTLE

Stachys bullata, S. rigida

California Hedge Nettle

Features: Have you ever walked along a river, stream, or swamp and smelled something mysterious, pungent yet pleasant, elusive and lemony? If you have, you were probably smelling hedge nettle. Highly aromatic hedge nettle is a little-known member of the mint family with a typical square stem and alternating pairs of opposite leaves. Most species of hedge nettle are perennials. Their lovely pale mauve flowers are 2-lipped and irregular, growing in whorled tiers at the tips of stalk and branches. They usually bloom from March to May, and then from midsummer to late summer. Although these somewhat sprawling plants may grow as tall as 2 feet high, they often go unnoticed, surrounded as they are by the much taller cattails and bulrushes of their swampy habitat.

Soft, fuzzy hairs cover their stems and heart-shaped, scallop-margined leaves. If you touch any part of this plant, the scent will linger on your hand. *Stachys palustris*, a similar species, which has pale rose flowers and oblong to lanceolate leaves, is also sometimes called hedge nettle, but more often is referred to as betony or marsh woundwort.

Facts: Hedge nettle can be found near other swamp plants in moist, shady locations below 2,000 feet throughout the West. Poultices used to stop bleeding and promote healing can be made from all species of hedge nettle by soaking the leaves in water for a few minutes. Infusions of hedge nettle leaves are used as a wash for wounds. All the species of this genus produce edible tubers. In Asia and Japan some species are cultivated, and their tubers, which are called "Chinese artichokes," are sold in markets. Here in the United States, hedge nettle tubers taste best when gathered in early autumn.

FOODS

Tea: Because the leaves are strong, steep only 1 leaf in 12 ounces of water for 5 minutes. Remove the leaf and serve. Young, spring leaves are slightly milder. It is said that hedge nettle tea relieves internal inflammation.

Raw: Tubers gathered in early autumn may be eaten raw.

Cooked: The tubers can be roasted or boiled, much like potatoes. Hedge nettle leaves are fuzzy and strong flavored, but the base of the stem is moist and crunchy.

HENBIT

Lamium amplexicaule

Dead Nettle

Features: Henbit is a small, unbranched winter annual or perennial member of the mint family only 4 to 12 inches high. It has several short, square stems to each root. Slightly hairy, almost circular, scallop-margined leaves grow opposite each other in pairs. Each leaf grows on a tiny stem. As the leaves near the top of this tiny herb, they begin to form tiers and clasp the stalk directly. In spring, 6 to 10 lovely, little, magenta-colored flowers appear in whorled clusters, growing between the tiered leaves. They bloom from April until August if they receive sufficient water.

Facts: Henbit grows in nearly all soils throughout North America. It is often called dead nettle because its leaves look like miniature nettle leaves, and its soft hairs resemble stinging nettle's painful hairs. Even though henbit is more a food extender than a food source due to its small size, because the plants grow in large groups it is often possible to gather a reasonable amount at one time. In Scandinavia, people have been eating henbit for centuries. The young plants, which are rich in vitamin C and have a light, minty flavor, often appear in early spring and can be gathered at any time because henbit is so mild.

FOODS
Tea: Put 2 tablespoons of fresh leaves or 1 teaspoon of dried leaves in a mug. Add boiling water, cover, and steep for 10 minutes. Strain and serve. Henbit tea has a mild, pleasant flavor.

Raw: Young leaves and stems, picked before the plant blooms, can be added to salads and sandwiches but usually are more enjoyable cooked because of their slightly fuzzy texture. The flowers can also be eaten raw.

Cooked: The whole plant can be added to omelettes.

HENBIT OMELETTE
Serves 2
> ½ cup water
> 2 tablespoons
>   henbit leaves
> ½ cup lamb's
>   quarters leaves
> 1 tablespoon butter
> 3 eggs
> 1 tablespoon milk

Bring the water to a boil. Add the leaves. Cover and steam at a low temperature for 2 to 3 minutes. Drain the leaves and set aside. Meanwhile, melt the butter. Scramble the eggs and milk together, and add to the butter. As the eggs are browning, add the greens. Fold the eggs over, then flip and brown the other side. Serve with hot, crusty sourdough bread.

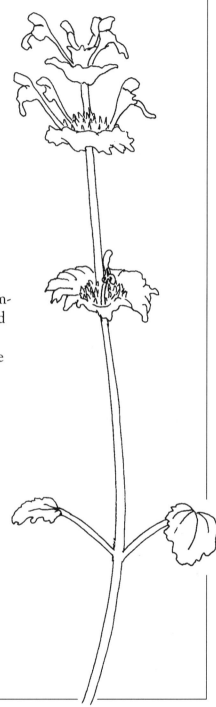

HIBISCUS

Hibiscus spp.

Features: Hibiscus is a hardy, annual shrub which has rapidly become a popular ornamental in the Southwest because of its attractive, evergreen foliage, spectacular flowers, and heat-tolerant nature. Hibiscus shrubs are bushy and usually grow about 6½ feet high unless trimmed, although some species can grow as high as 30 feet. Their large, glossy, green leaves are oval with deeply scalloped to slightly toothed margins and a pointed tip. Each leaf grows on a long individual stem, and the leaves shimmer and dance whenever the wind blows. There are over 300 species of hibiscus around the world, and large, lovely, flared hibiscus flowers with their 5 overlapping petals come in a variety of colors: purplish-red, red, orange, yellow, pink, and white; there is also an exotic white blossom which is rich red at the base of each petal. The flowers have conspicuous stamens surmounted by colorful yellow anthers. Although they are said to bloom during summer, in southern California these flowers bloom nearly year-round. Hibiscus flowers only last for a day or two, but when one dies, there is always a new one to take its place.

Facts: Originally from Africa, many varieties of hibiscus are cultivated in diverse tropical regions. These shrubs do not grow well in frost, but they thrive in full sun and well-drained soil. All hibiscus flowers are edible, but only the red ones are used medicinally. People who lived in the biosphere in Arizona suggest adding hibiscus leaves and flowers to bathwater to treat some skin conditions. For headaches and fevers, they mashed the leaves and applied them to their heads. Some people believe that eating iron-rich hibiscus leaves can bring relief to women who are experiencing a painful menstrual period. Summer is the best time to gather the flowers.

FOODS
Tea: Put 1 tablespoon of fresh petals or 1 teaspoon of dried petals in a cup. Add boiling water, cover, and steep for 5 minutes. Strain and drink as is or sweeten.

Raw: All hibiscus flowers can be eaten raw, and they make a colorful addition to salads and other foods. Their mild flavor is slightly tart.

HIBISCUS SUSHI
Based on a recipe from *Edible Flowers from Garden to Palate* by Cathy Wilkinson Barash.
Serves 6–8
> 1 cup sticky rice, cooked
> 1–2 tablespoons soy sauce
> 8 hibiscus flowers, pink or red
> 2 scrambled eggs, cut into strips, or
>   4 ounces smoked salmon, cut into strips
> 1 avocado, cut into strips
> Lettuce

Combine the rice and soy sauce. Clean and lay out the hibiscus flowers. Put 1 tablespoon of rice on each. Then put a strip of eggs or salmon and a strip of avocado in the center of the rice. Roll, refrigerate, and serve on a bed of lettuce.

HOLLY-LEAVED CHERRY

Prunus ilicifolia

Islay

Features: Evergreen holly-leaved cherry is a large shrub or small tree which grows from 8 to 30 feet high. It has gray to reddish-brown bark, shiny, green, prickly, holly-like leaves, and dangling racemes of tiny, white cherry blossoms and/or fruits. The drupes, or cherries, grow suspended, singly or in small clusters. Initially yellow-green in color, they become red or dull purplish-red when mature. Holly-leaved cherries are sweet, about the size of a gumball, and contain a single, very large seed. Holly-leaved cherry is sometimes confused with holly-leaved coffeeberry, *Rhamnus ilicifolia*, because of the similarity of their leaves and the fact that they both have white flowers. However, their fruits are very different. Coffeeberries are round, soft, and dark, becoming almost black when ripe.

Facts: *Prunus* is the genus of the trees in the rose family which produce stone-bearing fruit. Cherry, plum, peach, apricot, and almond trees all belong to this genus. Holly-leaved cherry can be found growing on dry slopes, alluvial fan beds, and especially in chaparral communities from southern California down into Mexico at elevations under 5,000 feet. Because there is very little flesh on holly-leaved cherries, sometimes the entire fruit was ground and used as meal by Native Americans. Even though the large cherry pits of holly-leaved cherry contain cyanide, Native Americans used to eat them as well as the pulp, but only after careful preparation. First the pits were dried in the sun. Then they were cracked open, and the kernels were removed to be crushed or ground. The resulting meal was leached in running water for several hours. Afterward it was cooked into mush or dried and made into patties which were roasted and stored for future use. Cahuillas boiled the leached kernels and used them in soup. Holly-leaved cherry pits were fermented and made into an intoxicating drink. The best time to gather these cherries is when they mature, which may be as early as June or as late as October.

Warning: If you wait for the cherries to ripen on the tree, you may be in for a major disappointment. Birds will get there first every time. Your best bet is to pick them just before they are ripe and let them continue ripening at home. Do not eat the cherry pits since they contain cyanide, a deadly poison.

FOODS

Tea: Holly-leaved cherry bark is sometimes made into a tea, which is used as a cold remedy. However, this is not a good idea because you damage the tree when you remove its bark.

Raw: The cherries can be eaten right off the tree, or they can be pressed and made into a drink. They range in flavor from bitter to sweet.

Cooked: A sweet sauce can be made from holly-leaved cherries.

WILD CHERRY SAUCE

2 cups holly-leaved cherries	Lemon juice
1 cup water	Sugar or honey to taste

Bruise the cherries, then put them in a pot. Add water. Bring to a boil, then simmer until the water is flavored. Strain and add lemon juice and sugar or honey to taste. Serve over ice cream or yogurt.

HOREHOUND

Marrubium vulgare

Concha, Soldier's Tea, Common Horehound

Features: A hardy perennial, horehound is a mat-like plant with several to a dozen square stems rising from each rootstock, giving the plants an almost bushy appearance, even though the stalks are unbranched. At times, these stems appear nearly white in color because they are covered with a white, fuzzy down. The heart-shaped leaves, which have toothed margins, are also covered with down. They appear darker in color than the stems and are distinctly crinkled over their entire surface. Mint-like, they grow in alternate pairs along the stalks. Although horehound plants can grow up to 2 feet tall, they are usually considerably shorter. It is said that horehound plants that grow in full sun are paler than those that grow in the shade. Horehound has tiny white flowers, which do not appear until its second year of growth. From spring through summer, they can be found growing in tiered whorls between the topmost pairs of leaves. After the flowers fall off, stiff whorls, containing seeds, remain. These are the prickly little hitchhikers which accompany you home after a stroll in the brush.

Facts: Although it is a native of Europe, by the 1900s horehound was widespread throughout the United States, growing in fields, chaparral, and waste places. The Latin name for horehound, *Marrubium*, comes from the Hebrew word *marrob*, which means bitter. This is no accident since the plant is so bitter that when I cooked my first batch of horehound candy my pot retained a bitter flavor for months afterwards, despite numerous cleanings. Many people use horehound medicinally, after it is sweetened. In Europe, it has even been used as a substitute for hops when brewing beer. Native Americans of Santa Ysabel, California, brewed a horehound tea which they used to treat colds and whooping cough. Navajos soaked horehound plants in water, and then drank the liquid as a cure for sore throats, coughs, stomachaches, and influenza. Even the ancient Egyptians used horehound as a cough medicine. Cahuillas made an infusion of it which they drank to flush the kidneys. Moreover, horehound can be used in a spray said to get rid of cankerworms in trees and to kill flies. Some people add horehound leaves to fresh milk and leave the bowl out to attract unwary 6-legged victims. The best time to gather young leaves for tea is in spring before the plants flower.

Warning: Prolonged use of horehound may contribute to high blood pressure, and high doses are laxative in nature.

FOODS
Tea: For a horehound infusion, Euell Gibbons, in *Stalking the Healthful Herbs*, suggests boiling 1 cup of fresh leaves or ½ cup of dried leaves in 2 cups of water for 10 minutes then letting it stand for 10 minutes before straining and sweetening it. For a milder-flavored drink, I pour 1 pint of boiling water over a

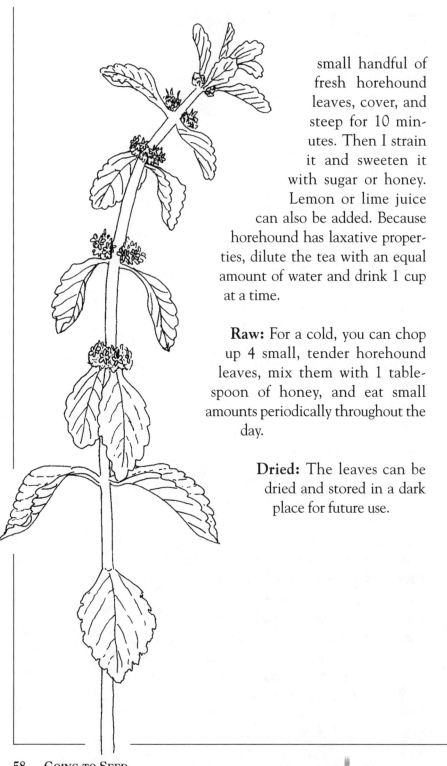

small handful of fresh horehound leaves, cover, and steep for 10 minutes. Then I strain it and sweeten it with sugar or honey. Lemon or lime juice can also be added. Because horehound has laxative properties, dilute the tea with an equal amount of water and drink 1 cup at a time.

Raw: For a cold, you can chop up 4 small, tender horehound leaves, mix them with 1 tablespoon of honey, and eat small amounts periodically throughout the day.

Dried: The leaves can be dried and stored in a dark place for future use.

HOREHOUND DROPS
Makes about a 6-inch square before cutting
   2 cups water
   ½ cup horehound leaves,
      cleaned and chopped
   Sugar or honey
   ⅛ teaspoon cream of tartar

Boil the water and leaves for no more than 5 minutes. Strain out the leaves and measure the remaining liquid. Stir in twice as much sugar or an equal amount of honey as liquid. Add the cream of tartar and mix well. Bring to a hard boil and continue boiling until the liquid reaches 290 degrees, checking the temperature with a candy thermometer. Pour immediately onto a buttered dish and fill your pot with water. When the candy begins to set, in 2 or 3 minutes, cut into small squares before it hardens. Meanwhile, if the syrup residue has irrevocably hardened in your cooking pot despite your best efforts, use hot water to dissolve it.

ICEPLANT

Mesembryanthemum crystallinum

Features: There are several members of the succulent carpet-weed family commonly known as iceplant. However, *Mesembryanthemum crystallinum* is the true iceplant. Spreading like a sparkling carpet over dry ground, this annual is easy to recognize. The small, succulent, dull green, oval- to spatulate-shaped leaves are somewhat curled and have smooth margins which are sometimes edged in red. Both the leaves and the thick, flexible, fleshy prostrate stems are adorned with numerous transparent water bubbles. Its tiny reddish flower buds and white flowers are present from March to October. Sea fig, *Carpobrotus aequilaterus*, a trailing, branched perennial with magenta or rose-red flowers which can grow over 3 feet in length but seems much longer because of its mat-like appearance, and the similar Hottentot fig, *C. edulis*, which has pale yellow flowers, are both mistakenly called iceplant.
However, they have no water bubbles, their daisy-like flowers are large, and their leaves differ significantly from the official iceplant. Both sea fig and Hottentot fig have long, narrow, curved, fleshy, 3-sided leaves which are wider than a pencil, can grow up to 4 inches long, and bloom from April to August

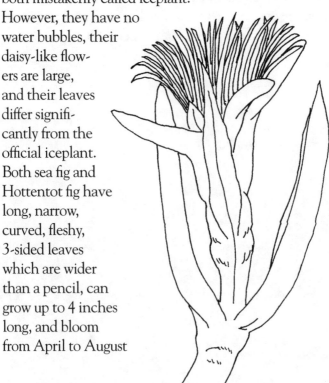

or September. Irregularly shaped fruits, about the size of large olives, form beneath the flowers of sea fig and Hottentot fig plants.

Facts: Iceplant, sea fig, and Hottentot fig all grow in the sunny, saline locations of temperate areas worldwide. Because they are so easy to grow, these African plants and similar species have become very popular since their introduction to our country. In the Southwest they are widespread, especially on coastal dunes. Although all three plants form thick mats, they are shallow-rooted and give way easily after heavy rains. Therefore, they cannot be recommended to prevent soil erosion. Dead iceplants add salt to the soil, provide good ground cover, and often prove exceptionally prolific.

FOODS

Raw: The fruit of the sea fig and Hottentot fig can be gathered throughout the summer after the flowers fall off. Iceplant's leaves and stems are most tender in spring. Mexicans eat the fruits of sea fig and Hottentot fig plants right from the plant. The milder-flavored iceplant is also edible, but not as popular as sea fig and Hottentot fig. Its tender young leaves and stems, which are salty and crunchy, can be eaten raw in salads and served with ranch dressing.

Cooked: Because sea fig and Hottentot fig leaves are so firm and crunchy, they are a good substitute for cucumbers in pickle recipes. Remember to cut back on the amount of salt called for in the recipe because these leaves are already very salty. The iceplant referred to in the following recipes is Hottentot or sea fig. Both are courtesy of Larry Palomera, who is from Guadalajara, Mexico. Iceplant can also be used, but the fruit is smaller, making it impractical.

GUADALAJARA ICEPLANT TORTILLAS

Makes 5–6 tortillas

> ½ cup iceplant fruit,
>   peeled and mashed
> ½ cup cornmeal
> 1 tablespoon oil
> Pinch salt
> A few drops
>   of lime juice

Combine all the ingredients in a bowl or blender. Form tortillas and grill.

OAXACA ICEPLANT SALSA
Makes about 3 cups

    8 tomatoes, chopped
    ½ onion, chopped
    3 cloves garlic, minced
    3–6 jalapeño peppers, sliced
    1 cup iceplant fruit, peeled and crushed
    ¼ cup fresh cilantro, chopped
    Salt
    3 or 4 crickets per tortilla (optional)

Cook the first 4 ingredients together. Mix with the fruit, cilantro, and salt. For a smoother salsa, use a blender. Eat with tortillas. Crickets can be added live to the tortillas or cooked in the salsa. Larry says that they're not bad, and a bit salty.

JERUSALEM ARTICHOKE

Helianthus tuberosus

Sunchoke, Sunflower Artichoke, Sunflower Root,
Wild Sunflower, Canada Potato

Features: The Jerusalem artichoke is a native perennial sunflower
which grows from 3 to 10 feet tall. It has large, simple, coarse,
gritty, ovate leaves which are longer and more pointed than other
sunflower leaves. Although these leaves grow in alternate pairs
near the base of the plant, higher up they are smaller and tend to
grow alternately but not in pairs. The erect stalk, which is covered with short, stiff, white hairs, branches slightly near the top.
In spring, the stalk and each branch are crowned by lovely,
golden yellow, daisy-like flowerheads 2 to 3 inches across. Sunflower blossoms appear to be made up of a center and petals, but
the petals are actually individual ray flowers. Unlike most other
sunflowers, Jerusalem artichokes do not have brown disk flowers
in their centers, nor do they produce copious quantities of large
edible seeds. Instead, their centers are filled with yellow disk flowers. They are also characterized by their edible tubers, which grow
from 3 to 5 inches long and up to 2 to 3 inches in diameter.

Facts: Jerusalem artichokes can be found growing in moist, open,
or roadside locations throughout the United States and Canada.
Although this plant is not really an artichoke, its tubers do taste
like a cross between potatoes and artichokes. It is the only sunflower to bear such large tubers, although they are short.
Jerusalem artichokes used to be cultivated by Native Americans
in the East and by settlers in Virginia. French colonists introduced them to Europe. In Italy this plant was called *girasole*,
which means "turning towards the sun." In Spain it was called
girasol, and later Anglicized to "Jerusalem." Jerusalem artichokes
are high in vitamin A and have many medicinal uses. The leaves
were used to combat malaria, and a tincture made from the blossoms was utilized to treat bronchitis. The roots were dried,

pounded, and chewed to relieve sore throats. Because these roots, which lack starch, are easy to digest and more nutritious than potatoes, they are often recommended as a gentle food for children, the elderly, and convalescents. Jerusalem artichokes provided an important food source for Native Americans, who boiled, baked, or fried the tubers. These plants propagate rapidly. If you find a single plant in your yard one day, do not be surprised to find it surrounded by others later. This situation may get out of hand, but remember: if you can't beat them, you can always eat them. Most people gather their tubers in fall and spring, but in colder climates the tubers reputedly taste better after a frost.

FOODS

Raw:
Crunchy Jerusalem artichoke tubers can be eaten raw after being cleaned and peeled. They are good cut into cubes and added to salads or served simply with salad dressing.

Cooked: The tubers, or "sunchokes" as they are known commercially, can be cooked just like potatoes, but because they contain no starch, their texture is more watery. They can be cleaned and simmered in a little water until they are tender, then served with butter and salt or salad dressing. They can also be partially cooked and then pickled. Sunchokes have a pleasant flavor which many people find sweet.

SCALLOPED SUNCHOKES
Serves 2

2 tablespoons butter	3 cups sunchokes, cooked
¼ cup flour	Salt and cayenne pepper
2 cups milk	3 tablespoons Parmesan cheese
¾ cup cheddar cheese, grated	

Melt the butter in a frying pan. Add the flour and stir until smooth. Slowly add the milk; then gradually add the cheddar cheese. Add the sunchokes and season to taste with salt and pepper. Pour into a glass baking dish and sprinkle with Parmesan cheese. Bake at 350 degrees for ½ hour or until done.

JOJOBA

Simmondsia chinensis

Goat Nut, Deer Nut

Features: Jojoba is a small, drought-tolerant, evergreen shrub. Jojoba bushes are hardy and have been known to live as long as 100 years on as little as 8 to 14 inches of rainfall per year. These densely branched schrubs can grow up to 7 feet tall but usually are much shorter. The branches are covered with numerous pairs of small yellow-green to blue-green, smooth-surfaced, smooth-margined, leathery leaves. Most of these leaves are positioned vertically so that their edges rather than their surfaces are exposed to the sun, thus minimizing water loss. On separate plants there are tiny, yellow male flowers, or tiny, inconspicuous, greenish female flowers which are followed by large, green, attractive, filbert-sized capsules, each containing 2 small nuts the size of pine nuts. In August and September, when the thin green covering of the capsules begins to turn brown and wither, the nuts fall out.

Facts: Jojoba grows on dry slopes and along hillside washes on well-drained soil in the southern Mojave and Sonoran Deserts at elevations below 5,000 feet. Jojoba nuts contain

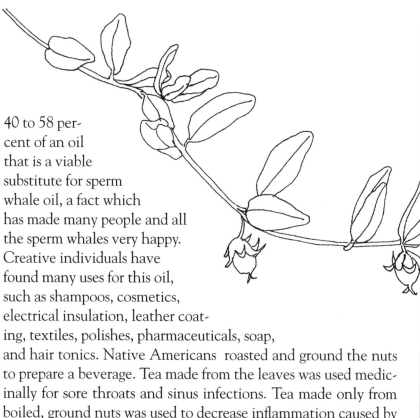

40 to 58 per-
cent of an oil
that is a viable
substitute for sperm
whale oil, a fact which
has made many people and all
the sperm whales very happy.
Creative individuals have
found many uses for this oil,
such as shampoos, cosmetics,
electrical insulation, leather coating, textiles, polishes, pharmaceuticals, soap,
and hair tonics. Native Americans roasted and ground the nuts
to prepare a beverage. Tea made from the leaves was used medicinally for sore throats and sinus infections. Tea made only from
boiled, ground nuts was used to decrease inflammation caused by
sore throats. Chewing on the raw green nuts was also supposed to
help. Moreover, Native Americans utilized jojoba oil as a hair
tonic to treat brittle hair and dry scalp, and a shampoo was made
by grinding the nuts. The best time to gather the nuts is in August
and September when the capsules begin to turn brown and
wither.

Warning: Jojoba nuts contain tannic acid and can be harmful if consumed in
large quantities.

FOODS
Raw: Jojoba nuts are tasty eaten right off the bush, but a few go a
long way because they are so rich in oil. Although some people
consider them bitter, I find them very pleasant even when they
have been sitting around for several weeks.

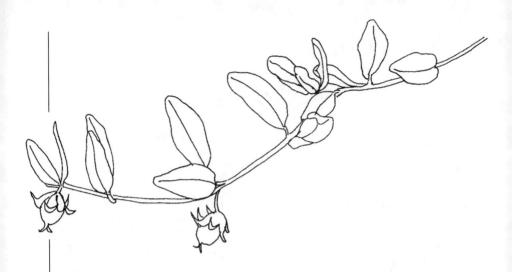

Cooked: To roast the nuts, place them on an ungreased cookie sheet in the oven at 250 to 275 degrees for about 1 hour, stirring occasionally. You can sprinkle them with salt, eat them plain, or use them to prepare a beverage. Early Californians roasted the nuts and then ground them together with hard-boiled egg yolks. The resulting mixture was boiled in water for several minutes before milk, sugar, and vanilla were added. Sometimes the ground nuts were simply boiled with milk and sugar. Cahuillas ground the nuts and boiled them in water, then removed the nuts and drank the liquid.

Green Beans with Jojoba Nuts
Serves 2–3

1 tablespoon butter	2 cups green beans
2 tablespoons jojoba nuts, chopped	¼ cup water

Melt the butter and sauté the nuts until coated. Add the beans and water. Cook over medium heat, stirring occasionally, for about 5 minutes or until done.

OATMEAL SUPREME
Serves 2–3

2 cups water	6 tablespoons raisins
Pinch of salt	4 tablespoons jojoba nuts
1 cup steel cut oats	1 teaspoon cinnamon

Bring the water and salt to a boil. Combine the other ingredients in a bowl and slowly add them to the water, stirring constantly. Cover and turn down the heat. Continue to stir occasionally, cooking for 5 minutes or until done. Sweeten to taste and serve with milk if desired.

JUNIPER

Juniperus spp.

Features: There are many species of juniper, ranging from small spreading shrubs to trees 20 feet tall. All junipers are aromatic, evergreen, and bear hard berry-like cones which are green their first year but turn blue-black in their second or third year when they ripen. Junipers do not actually produce seeds until they are about 10 years old. Their leaves range from small and needle-like to scale-like. The often shreddy, sometimes thin, bark is aromatic. Although all species produce edible berries, some taste better than others.

Facts: Junipers usually grow on dry, sunny slopes, in shady areas, and in dry, rocky locations often near piñon trees. The many species of juniper can be found at higher elevations throughout the Southwest. Juniper berries were an important year-round food source for Native Americans. They are most abundant between June and August but keep well for long periods of time. Only the mature, blue-black berries should be gathered. Some trees produce juniper berries every year, but the rest of the trees produce berries every other year. Perhaps raw juniper berries are an acquired taste. Numerous Native Americans seem to relish them, while some of us find them a bit strong. Raw juniper berries were chewed to cure colds and fevers and to stimulate the digestion. Damp, steaming juniper branches were applied to ease arthritis, rheumatism, and aching joints. Sometimes these branches were wrapped in wet cloths. Tea made from 1 teaspoon of dried leaves and berries was used to treat bladder infections. Juniper is said to have diuretic properties, and this tea is also reputed to be good for kidney ailments. Aromatic juniper leaves can be burned as incense, and juniper branches were burned both as incense and as a disinfectant. The ashes, mixed with water, were used by the Hopis to flavor their food, as well as to color well-known piki bread (blue tortillas) and make it rise. Shreddy juniper bark was used to make clothes or stuff mattresses. Today, Navajos still dry juniper berries and use them to make necklaces.

Warning: Drink juniper tea in moderation since it is diuretic.

FOODS

Tea: Heat 10 young juniper sprigs in 1 quart of water until the water begins to boil. Turn down the heat and simmer for 15 minutes. For a milder tea, add boiling water to the sprigs. Cover and steep for 10 minutes. This tea is sometimes used to cure constipation and is utilized by Navajo women to regain strength after giving birth.

Raw: The mature blue-black berries can be eaten raw. Eating a few an hour before a meal is said to aid digestion.

Cooked: Juniper berries can be roasted, ground, and added to cornmeal, or used as a flavoring for sauerkraut, potato salad, game, meat, vegetables, and various other dishes. They can also be roasted, ground, and brewed into a hot drink. In addition to the following recipe, juniper berries are also included as an ingredient in Marinated and Broiled Sulfur Shelf Fungus with Flank Steak (page 177).

DELICIOUS BAKED CABBAGE WITH JUNIPER
Serves 4–6

1 medium-sized cabbage	6 mature juniper berries,
1 tablespoon olive oil	crushed
1 onion, chopped	¼ to ⅓ cup water
1 clove garlic, minced	Salt and cayenne pepper

Remove the center core from the cabbage and mince the remainder. Heat the oil in an ovenproof frying pan. Slowly sauté the onion and garlic until clear. Stir in the berries. Then add the cabbage, water, and seasoning. Cover and bake at 350 degrees for 35 minutes or until done.

MARIPOSA LILY, SEGO LILY

Calochortus spp.

Star Tulip, Butterfly Tulip, Cat's Ear

Features: There are 60 species of *Calochortus*. Usually perennial, these lilies are small, delicate plants typically under 1 foot in height, although they can grow taller. Their slender stem, which sometimes branches sparsely near the top, rises from a coated bulb which grows 5 to 6 inches beneath the ground. Sego lily bulbs are rarely over 1 inch in diameter and are attached by a thin thread which breaks easily when disturbed. Narrow, grass-like leaves grow at the base of the plant, but they begin to wither about the time the large, showy, white, cream-colored, yellow, orange, pink, scarlet, mauve, or purple flowers appear. These attractive, 3-petaled, tulip-like flowers can be as large as 3 inches in diameter. They grow singly or in small terminal clusters of 2 to 4 and generally bloom from May to August. Mariposa lilies are characterized by a gland which has the appearance of a dark spot at the base of each petal. In different species these spots vary in shape, color, and presence of soft hairs. Surprisingly, they only bloom every 2 or 3 years because they require time to store up the necessary energy.

Facts: Both mariposa and sego lilies prefer partial shade and can be found growing in open spaces, plains, and meadows throughout the West at elevations below 10,500 feet. The name *mariposa* means butterfly in Spanish. All parts of butterfly tulips are edible. The bulbs, which are also known as corms, were an important food source for Native Americans and early pioneers. During the fall of 1848, when a horde of crickets destroyed the crops at settlements in Utah, Mormon settlers would have starved without sego lily bulbs to eat. In gratitude, Utah's citizens elected to make the sego lily, *Calochortus nuttallii*, their state flower. Although sego lily bulbs are not easy to gather, Native Americans managed to harvest the bulbs in large quantities, using digging sticks which were pointed and tempered at one end. They dried the bulbs and later pounded them into flour to make mush. They also collected the seeds and ground them for food. Corms are usually gathered when the flowers first appear in spring.

Warning: Many of these species are endangered so only pick them in an emergency. If you want to sample a corm, collect one where there are plenty of plants.

FOODS
Raw: Mariposa lily and sego lily corms can be eaten raw; some people prefer them salted. The flowers and flower buds can be added to salads.

Cooked: Mariposa lily and sego lily corms can be cooked in any way you would cook potatoes. They taste especially good when roasted in a pit. The entire plant can be cooked like a potherb.

Dried: Mariposa lily and sego lily corms can be dried and stored for future use.

MARIPOSA BULBS O'BRIAN
Serves 2–3
>1 tablespoon butter
>½ onion, chopped
>4 tablespoons green onions chopped
>1 cup mariposa lily bulbs chopped
>Salt and cayenne pepper

Melt the butter. Stir in the onions and cook until clear. Add the chopped bulbs and stir until coated with onions and butter. Season to taste with salt and pepper, cover, and continue cooking for 5 more minutes, adding a little water when necessary.

MILK THISTLE

Silybum marianum

Variegated Thistle, St. Mary's Thistle

Features: Milk thistle is a large, handsome, much-branched annual or biennial spring plant which grows up to 6 feet tall if it receives sufficient water. This extremely hardy and prolific plant is characterized by unusually large, shiny, lovely leaves which are decorated by a striking network of milk-white veins. These deeply lobed leaves are surprisingly tender for leaves of their size, even though they have sharp thistle spines at the tips of each of their many lobes and smaller spines along their margins. Milk thistle blooms from May to July. Its lovely purple flowerheads grow up to 2 inches in diameter, and are encircled by an attractive multilay-ered collar of stiff, pointed, leaf-like bracts, each of which terminates in a sharp spine. In the center of each flowerhead are several minute white disk flowers. Tall, upright, grooved stalks look as if they are dusted with white powder.

Facts: Milk thistle can be found growing in weedy areas and waste places, especially where there is some moisture such as along irrigation ditches and near streams. It is common in many regions of the world, including areas of California, Arizona, and New Mexico. All parts of all thistles are edible, although the roots taste best when picked before the flower stalk appears, and the leaves are always more tender and less bitter if they are picked in spring before the flowers bloom. The seeds mature by late summer. Milk thistle leaves are the mildest, tastiest, and most tender of all the thistle leaves I have eaten. Moreover, science is discovering that this plant has great medical potential. Since 1859 milk thistles have been used to treat liver and spleen disorders, hypertension, and other physical problems. Because of its restorative effect on the liver, it is currently being considered as an antidote for death cap mushroom poisoning. Sometimes milk thistle is included in homeopathic remedies for internal cleansing. Do not hesitate to ask for permission to pick prolific milk thistle; most park rangers are overjoyed to comply.

FOODS

Raw: The leaves can be eaten raw after the spines have been cut off with scissors. Young milk thistle leaves are tender, but they become tough as they mature.

Cooked: Young milk thistle leaves can be boiled for 10 minutes, then drained and served with butter, sauce, or lemon juice. Unopened buds can be cooked like artichokes, but because they are quite a bit smaller, they do not provide much food.

CREAM OF MILK THISTLE SOUP
Serves 2

1 tablespoon butter	1 cup milk
2 cloves garlic, minced	½ teaspoon thyme
1 onion, sliced	Salt and cayenne pepper
1 cup water	Parmesan cheese
1 cup milk thistle leaves, washed and chopped	

Melt the butter and sauté the garlic and onion until clear. Add the water and bring to a boil. Next add the milk thistle and continue boiling until the leaves are tender, about 5 minutes. Add the milk and turn down the heat. Do not bring the mixture to a boil. Then add the thyme, salt, and pepper. Sprinkle with Parmesan cheese before serving. This delicious soup is great served with hot, crusty sourdough bread.

MOUNTAIN GERANIUM

Geranium spp.

Features: Perennial mountain geraniums look like a cross between domestic geraniums and stork's bill, *Erodium* spp. They can grow up to 2 feet tall, and although they are usually upright, occasionally they support themselves on nearby plants. Dull green, slightly fuzzy mountain geranium leaves are deeply cleft with 3 to 5 lobes which are subdivided into 3 parts each. These leaves grow singly on long leaf stems or along the flower stalks. Five-petaled flowers, which bloom in early summer, range in color from white to mauve and grow singly or in small clusters. Some are decorated with delicate, vertical, dark red lines. Mature flowers are replaced by long, slender, needle-like seedpods which form spirals when they are ready to leave the plants. Mountain geranium's leaves resemble those of larkspur, *Delphinium glaucum*, and monkshood, *Aconitum columbianum*, which are poisonous plants. But once the plants bloom, their differences are obvious. Both larkspur and monkshood flowers join together in the back, and larkspur's petals form a spur. Their flowers are a deep, unforgettable bluish-purple.

Facts: Mountain geraniums grow in moist, mountainous locations. Although they are not choice, mountain geraniums are edible. Ingenious Native Americans discovered medicinal uses for mountain geranium. They combined the powdered roots with water and used them to treat dysentery, internal hemorrhaging, and to dry up slowly-healing sores. Poultices made from the crushed roots were utilized to treat protruding piles, arthritis, and sore feet. The dried leaves were used to make a mouthwash for sore throats. Tea made from the steeped roots was believed to provide birth control effective for up to an entire year.

Warning: Do not pick mountain geraniums until they flower to avoid confusing them with two poisonous plants: larkspur, *Delphinium glaucum*, which has similar leaves but strikingly different flowers, and monkshood, *Aconitum columbianum*. Both larkspur and monkshood have flowers which join at the back, and larkspur's petals form a spur.

FOODS

Raw: Both the leaves and flowers can be eaten as a pleasantly spicy snack or added to salads.

Cooked: Mountain geranium greens can be steamed, boiled as a potherb, or chopped and added to soups and stews.

MOUNTAIN GERANIUM PASTA SALAD

Serves 2–4

> 6 cups water
> 1 cup wide egg noodles
> ½ cup zucchini, diced
> ½ cup corn
> 3 tomatoes, cubed
> 3 tablespoons salad dressing
> 1 tablespoon mountain geranium
>   leaves, cleaned and diced
> Salt and cayenne pepper

Bring the water to a boil. Add the noodles and continue boiling, uncovered, for 3 minutes. Add the zucchini and corn. Continue cooking until the noodles are tender. Drain. Transfer to a salad bowl and mix with the tomatoes, dressing, and leaves. Season to taste with salt and pepper. Garnish with mountain geranium flowers.

SALAD DRESSING

Makes ½ cup

> 2 tablespoons extra-virgin olive oil
> 6 tablespoons lemon juice
> 1 clove garlic, crushed
> Salt and cayenne pepper

Combine the first 3 ingredients and season to taste with salt and pepper.

MOUNTAIN SORREL

Oxyria digyna

Features: Mountain sorrel is an alpine perennial. Although it is not in the *Rumex* genus, it has properties and uses similar to the *Rumex* sorrels. Both sorrels have erect, slightly branched stalks, small greenish-red flowers, and tiny, flat fruits encased in red, triangular paper-like coverings. One feature that sets mountain sorrel apart is its leaves. Unlike the large, long, often ruffled leaves of most of the docks and sorrels of the *Rumex* genus, the leaves of mountain sorrel are smaller, round to kidney-shaped, and each is supported by a long stem. Most of its leaves are basal, and both the leaves and the one or several flower stalks, which grow 6 to 12 inches tall, are joined to a single stout rootstock. In late summer mountain sorrel leaves begin to turn red. From July to September inconspicuous yellow-green to red flowers grow in whorled clusters on the stems and branches.

Facts: Mountain sorrel grows among rocks at high elevations throughout the world. In southern California and the Pacific Northwest, it can be found growing at elevations above 9,400 feet. It is considered a valuable plant, both for food and medicine. As you can guess from its sour flavor, mountain sorrel is high in vitamin C and in the past was one of the plants used to treat scurvy. Young sorrel leaves, which can be gathered in spring and sometimes in fall, reputedly stimulate the appetite, assist the kidneys, and aid digestion. Native Americans, especially those of Alaska and Canada, fermented sorrel leaves to make a sauerkraut. They also ground seeds, gathered in summer, to use as a seasoning, flour extender, or hot cereal. The leaves were steeped to make a refreshing spring tonic. This versatile plant can be used for a complexion-cleansing facial steam and is even a viable rennet substitute. In moderate climates mountain sorrel is available year-round.

Warning: Mountain sorrel contains oxalic acid, which combines with calcium to form calcium oxalate crystals in your body, especially in the kidneys. This depresses the level of calcium in body fluids. Older leaves contain more acid than younger ones; freezing or cooking helps to break down this toxin. Remember to eat sorrel in moderation, and only use the young leaves.

FOODS

Tea: A pleasant tea can be made by steeping a few leaves, covered, in boiling water for 10 minutes. The tea tastes slightly sour when served hot and very refreshing when chilled. This tea is said to help clear the complexion, and it can also be used as a mouthwash or gargle.

Raw: Young leaves and stems collected in spring can be used to spice up salads and sandwiches with their lemony flavor.

Cooked: The leaves are good boiled with meat or cooked like spinach, if you remember that they have a strong, lemony flavor. Young leaves can be used as a rhubarb substitute. Seeds can be gathered in late summer, ground, and added to flour or hot cereal. They also make a good snack.

Dried: Young, unblemished leaves can be picked in spring and dried for future use.

SUPER SORREL SOUP
Serves 4–6

1 tablespoon butter	¼ cup sorrel leaves, minced
4 cloves garlic, minced	2 cups milk
1 onion, chopped	Salt and cayenne pepper
4 sprigs thyme	2 cups yogurt or sour cream
2 cups water	

Melt the butter in a large pot. Sauté the garlic and onion until clear. Stir in the thyme and add the water. Cover and heat to a boil. Add the sorrel. Turn down the heat and continue cooking for about 5 more minutes or until the sorrel is tender. Add the milk and warm for a few minutes but do not boil. Season to taste with salt and pepper, then stir in the yogurt or sour cream. Serve immediately.

MULBERRY

Morus nigra

Black Mulberry

Features: Mulberry is a large, bushy, deciduous shrub or small tree which grows up to 15 feet tall. Attractive heart-shaped to irregularly lobed leaves grow alternately along slender, flexible branches. Each leaf has its own long stem, which allows it to dance gracefully in the slightest breeze. All of the leaves have serrated margins and come to a conspicuous point at their tips. Mulberry leaves are green above and paler underneath. Mulberry bark ranges from grayish-brown to warm reddish-brown, but it can appear soft rosy-orange on sunny days. Tiny greenish-white mulberry flowers are arranged in catkins and grow suspended beneath some of the leaves. As they mature and drop off, they are replaced by lumpy, irregularly shaped, somewhat oval, incredibly sweet mulberries, which grow about 1 inch long. Initially green, these luscious berries become a rich, purplish-black when ripe in summer. Under optimal conditions, the berries appear as early as April or May.

Facts: Mulberry trees grow in moist locations along streams and washes from western Texas to California and as far south as northern Mexico. White mulberry, *Morus alba*, is well known as the source of the mulberry leaves favored by silkworms. It is similar to the black mulberry except for its rugged, brownish-yellow bark and hairless leaves. Before the time of the American Revolution, American settlers brought white mulberry trees to the New World in an unsuccessful attempt to start a silk industry. Native to China, white mulberry trees are abundant in Lebanon and Israel and also grow in Iraq. Black mulberry juice was used medicinally to soothe sore throats or reduce high fevers. It has also been utilized as a sedative or mild narcotic. Large quantities of berries, and tea made from the boiled inner bark, have a mild laxative effect.

Warning: Do not eat uncooked shoots or unripe fruit of any variety of mulberry because they are all hallucinogenic.

FOODS

Raw: Ripe mulberries are delicious raw. They appear in summer and are dark red, deep purple, purplish-black, or black.

Cooked: Cooked ripe mulberries make excellent pies, flans, preserves, fruit soups, and can be combined with lemon or rhubarb juice. Young shoots can also be cooked.

Frozen: Mulberries freeze well and can be frozen plain, coated with sugar, or covered with syrup. Some people like to remove the cores before serving the thawed berries.

MULBERRY PIE
Serves 4–6
Crust:

1 cup flour	4 tablespoons butter
2–4 tablespoons ice water	

Prepare the crust: Combine the ingredients, roll out the crust, place it in a greased pie pan, and bake it at 375 degrees for 10 minutes. Remove it from the oven and set aside.

Filling:

3 cups ripe mulberries	¾ cup sugar
¼ cup lemon juice	1 tablespoon butter
3 tablespoons flour	2 tablespoons sugar (optional)

Gently combine the berries, juice, flour, and ¾ cup of sugar. Pour the mixture into the pie crust. Crumble the butter over the pie. (If you prefer a 2-crust pie, make a second crust and place it on top of the filling. Sprinkle it with 2 tablespoons of sugar.) Bake at 425 degrees for 10 minutes and then at 375 degrees for 25 minutes. Cool before serving, and top with whipped cream or vanilla ice cream if desired.

NARROW-LEAVED PLANTAIN

Plantago lanceolata

English Plantain, Ribwort

Features: Narrow-leaved plantain is an annual or biennial that starts out as a basal cluster of long, narrow leaves with prominent parallel ribs running along their length. Under optimal conditions, it can grow up to 2 feet tall, and the leaves can reach nearly 1 foot in length. Each leaf is supported by its own stem. One to several tall, slender, leafless flower stalks rise from the midst of the basal rosette of leaves. Both leaves and flower stalks are covered with fine white hairs. These upright stems are unbranched, and each is crowned by a soft, tiny, light brown, cone-like growth. From May to November, rings of tiny greenish-white flowers encircle the cone, first lower down, and then progressively closer to the tips. Because these flowers are on individual thread-like stems, sometimes the rings of flowers look like fragile halos floating atop the stalks. Eventually the flowers are replaced by small brown seeds which form dense spikes.

Facts: Narrow-leaved plantain grows almost anywhere but is especially abundant in open fields, chaparral, meadows, and yards. Plantain grows in moist places throughout the world, and there are 14 species of *Plantago* in California alone. They are all edible unless they are growing in polluted water or in locations which have been sprayed by pesticides. Plantains have several medicinal uses. Plantain leaves are high in vitamins A and C. Tea made from the leaves is slightly laxative in nature and has been used to treat eczema, skin disorders, coughs, hoarseness, and general respiratory problems. The seeds also serve as a mucilaginous laxative in the same manner as more potent psyllium seeds. The fresh leaves have been used as a poultice on leg ulcers, nettle stings, burns, abrasions, insect bites, snake bites, wounds, and hemorrhoids. Warmed, they have been applied to swollen glands to relieve the pain.

FOODS

Tea: Put ½ cup of chopped leaves in a mug. Add 1 cup of boiling water, cover, and steep for 10 minutes. The resulting tea is mild and slightly laxative in nature.

Raw: In spring, very young leaves, gathered before the flower stalks extend beyond the leaves, can be added to salads and sandwiches. However, after the flower stalks appear, the leaves become stringy.

Cooked: The young leaves can be chopped and steamed for 10 minutes to eat as a potherb, or they can be added to soups and stews.

Seeds: The seeds can be used as a laxative. Soak them in water for a while, then drink the liquid, seeds and all. The seeds can also be ground and used as a flour extender, snack, or cooked like rice.

SCALLOPED PLANTAIN
Serves 2

4 potatoes, scrubbed	2 cups milk
2 cups plantain leaves, cleaned and chopped	2 tablespoons white wine (optional)
2 tablespoons butter	Salt and cayenne pepper
4 tablespoons flour	1½ cups cheddar cheese, grated

Steam the potatoes in a pot for about 20 minutes or until tender. Remove them from the pot, but leave the water boiling. Add the plantain leaves. Cover and cook for 10 minutes. Drain and set aside. Melt the butter in a frying pan. Gradually add the flour, stirring constantly. Then add and blend in the milk, wine, and salt and pepper to taste, continuing to stir. Meanwhile, skin and slice the potatoes. Spread ½ of the potatoes in an ungreased baking pan. Put the plantain leaves on top. Then spread the remaining potatoes on top of the greens. Pour the sauce over everything. Sprinkle with cheddar cheese and bake at 375 degrees for 20 minutes.

NATAL PLUM

Carissa macrocarpa, C. grandiflora

Features: Natal plum is an attractive, ornamental, evergreen shrub which grows up to 2 feet in height. Its shiny, leathery, green leaves are oval with pointed tips and smooth margins. They are paler below than above and grow alternately along numerous spiny branches. Stunning, white, 5-petaled flowers grow in small bunches at the tips of the branches. Resembling the larger plumeria (*Plumeria rubra*) blossoms of Hawaii, which are used to make leis, they bloom at varied times and over an extended period. Like the plumeria, they are also aromatic. Natal plums are firm, about the size of small plums, and dark red when ripe. Both fruits and flowers can be seen growing on the bush at the same time. When a fruit is picked, its stout stem exudes a milky sap.

Facts: Originally from Africa, natal plums can grow in full sun or shade on a variety of soils and are often cultivated in subtropical areas. They also grow well in the Southwest. While natal plums are technically not wild plants, they are common ornamentals which produce copious supplies of firm, edible fruit. Mexicans love them, and so do children, although most gringos avoid them. This is probably due in part to the white sap. Although it is a common belief that any plant which has white sap is poisonous, obviously this is not true. Since natal plums are usually cultivated plants, remember to check if plants were sprayed with pesticides before eating the fruit. It is also important not to eat fruit or plants that grow too close to traffic, because they become contaminated by exhaust fumes of passing cars.

FOODS
Raw: When the natal plums are firm and deep red, they are ready to eat. The season they mature extends over much of the year, and in southern California may extend from spring through autumn. Many people find these plums delightful, whereas others, myself included, find them a bit astringent.

Cooked: Cooked natal plums make tasty jams, jellies, and sauces, which are an attractive rose-red.

NATAL PLUM JELLY

Based on a recipe in *Edible and Useful Plants of California*, by Charlotte Bringle Clarke.
Makes 4 cups

4 pounds ripe natal plums, washed
1 cup water

¼ cup lemon juice
1 package pectin
6 cups sugar

Crush the plums in a pot. Stir in the water and lemon juice. Cover and simmer for 15 minutes. Strain out the liquid and measure. Add water if necessary to increase the amount of liquid to total 4 cups. Return the juice to the pot and stir in the pectin. Bring to a boil and add the sugar, stirring constantly. Continue heating until the mixture reaches a full boil. Boil for 2 to 3 minutes, then pour the jelly into sterilized or freezer jars.

NAVAJO TEA

Thelesperma megapotamicum

Cota, Green Thread, Indian Tea

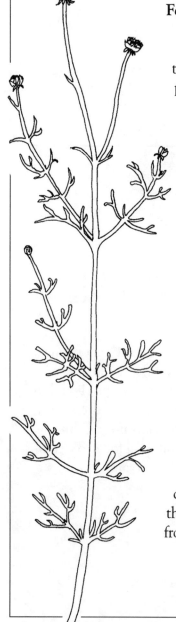

Features: It is easy to overlook Navajo tea plants the first time you search for them. Even though they grow from 1 to 2 feet tall, most of the surrounding grasses and plants are much larger and more conspicuous. They are very slender, with green, nodding, thread-like, slightly branched stems and long, grass-like leaves. From July to September, delicate yellow flowerheads appear. Later, after the flowers die, the entire plant becomes a faded shade of yellow-brown. Navajo tea is either annual, biennial, or perennial. Although young plants first appear around May, dry plants often remain until October.

Facts: Navajo tea can be found growing in Wyoming, Colorado, New Mexico, Utah, Arizona, and Mexico at elevations between 4,000 and 7,500 feet, on grassy plains, mesas, streambanks, dry slopes, in canyons, and open woodlands. It is used medicinally by many different Native Americans, including the Kiiyionnis, the Hopis, the Navajos, and the Apaches. Tea brewed from this plant is best known as a remedy for upset stomachs, but in the past it has also been utilized as a diuretic and to relieve heartburn and fevers. Many people believe that Navajo tea is good for the kidneys and has a purifying effect on the blood. It is best to collect this plant from July to September, when it blooms, so that you do not pick the wrong plant by mistake.

FOODS

Tea: Tea made from Navajo tea is delicious if prepared properly; otherwise it is bitter. First gather it into bundles about 4 or 5 inches long. Next rinse the bundles and secure them with a piece of string, then hang them in a dark, dry place. After at least two days, remove the amount of dried plant you wish to use. Boil 3 cups of water for each dried bundle of plants to be used. Add the plants, cover, and continue to boil for 5 minutes but no longer. The tea should be a lovely pale orange to pale red. It can be sweetened but tastes wonderful just as it is. Save the plants and use them again, in the same manner, for a milder tea. You do not need to wait for an upset stomach to enjoy this delicious brew.

NEW ZEALAND SPINACH

Tetragonia tetragonioides

Features: New Zealand spinach is a handsome, annual succulent. Except in unprotected locations, it spreads rapidly and can usually be found growing as a congested community of many spreading plants. Although these hardy plants are upright at first, they tend to become prostrate as they continue growing. Their large, dark green, fleshy leaves are triangular in shape with curled-under margins and grow up to 2 inches long. The stalks are also fleshy and covered with leaves. From April through September, tiny, solitary, yellow-green flowers grow nestled beneath the leaf stems where they meet the stalk. All parts of New Zealand spinach plants are covered with small, glistening droplets filled with fluid, which sparkle in the sun.

Facts: New Zealand spinach generally grows in the sandy soil of salt marshes and beaches along the coasts of Oregon and California, although it can occasionally be found growing in moist, shady environments. It is not a native of the United States but was imported from the Pacific, introduced to the public by Captain Cook. It is also a native of Southeast Asia and grows in Japan, Australia, and, of course, New Zealand. Currently being cultivated in South America, it has been grown in England since 1821 and in France since 1824. New Zealanders do not use it as a potherb, and very few people in the Southwest seem to appreciate it or even known what it is. However, hardy, attractive New Zealand spinach is a wonderful plant that not only tastes good but is far superior to domestic spinach. Once it gets started in a yard, it takes care of itself and provides an almost year-round supply of fresh greens. Most abundant from spring through autumn, New Zealand spinach is such a mild-flavored plant that it can be harvested anytime it is available.

FOODS

Raw: The crunchy leaves can be added to salads and sandwiches. They maintain their crispness far longer than most other greens.

Cooked: The leaves can be steamed, boiled, sautéed, stir-fried, or added to soups and stews, although it is necessary to allow a little more cooking time than you would for a more fragile plant. New Zealand spinach tastes good served with butter and/or lemon juice.

CREAM OF SPINACH SOUP
Serves 4

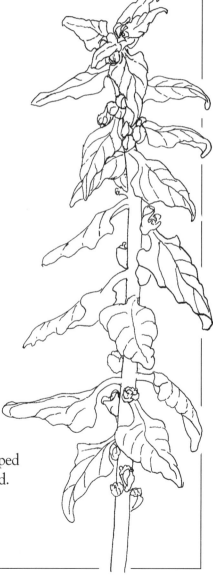

> 2 tablespoons butter
> 2 cloves garlic, minced
> 1 onion, chopped
> 1 potato, diced
> 2 cups water
> 2 cups New Zealand
>   spinach leaves,
>   cleaned and chopped
> 2 cups milk
> Salt and cayenne pepper
> ½ teaspoon thyme
> ½ cup sour cream (optional)

Sauté the garlic and onion in the butter until clear. Add the potato and water. Cover and boil for 10 minutes. Add the spinach leaves. Turn down the heat and simmer for 5 minutes more. Add the milk and seasonings. Heat but do not boil. Serve hot, topped with a dollop of sour cream, if desired.

OCOTILLO

Fouquieria splendens

Slimwood, Couchwhip, Candlewood

Features: It is hard to miss ocotillo when it is blooming. Usually growing in large, scattered groups, these unusual desert shrubs reach an impressive height of 6 to 20 feet. Woody, unbranched, whip-like stems join together at a shallow central root system. Tiny, bright green, spatulate-shaped leaves grow alternately along the length of the stems unless there is insufficient water, in which case they drop off. In spring, usually from April through May, the leaves are joined by brilliant reddish-orange flowers which grow along the terminal ends of the stems. Hidden among the leaves and flowers are sharp, slender, woody thorns. The amount of rainfall determines how many leaves the plants will bear, how soon they will bloom, and how abundant the flowers will be.

Facts: Ocotillos grow around desert valleys, rocky hillsides, and mesatops from the Colorado Desert of southeastern California to the Chihuahua Desert of Texas at altitudes ranging from sea level to 4,500 feet. Although ocotillos are legally protected by California and Arizona, they can still be collected in other locales. People in third world countries, such as Haiti and Mexico, often use ocotillos to create a living hedge. Such a hedge can be made by simply planting several stalks and watering them every day for a few weeks. In no time they will take root and soon provide an attractive, thorny fence that is not only good for keeping unwanted visitors out but is also useful for hanging laundry to dry. These straight, sturdy stalks have been used as torches in Mexico. Cahuillas make a strong tea from the roots to treat the moist, painful coughing of old people. Apaches also made a tea which they drank to combat fatigue. Ocotillo juice is thought to relieve pain and swelling, and powdered ocotillo root was sometimes used in the same manner. Bathing in water which contains powdered ocotillo root gave further relief from painful, swollen limbs and fatigue. The wax coating on the stalks was used to treat leather. Nutritious ocotillo seeds contain 29 percent protein and were an excellent food source for Native Americans. After the flowers wilted, the seeds were gathered, parched, and ground. Then the resulting flour was made into mush or formed into cakes and dried.

FOODS

Raw: The flowers can be eaten raw or made into a refreshing drink.

Cooked: The seeds can be parched and ground to make cakes, mush, or beverages.

OCOTILLO-ADE
Ocotillo blossoms
Water

Soak equal amounts of blossoms and water together for an hour or so. Or put the water and blossoms in a clear container and leave it in the sun for several hours.

OLIVE

Olea europaea

Features: Olive trees grow in a variety of shapes and sizes, ranging from picturesque gnarled trees with intriguing twisted branches to tall, stately shade trees which grow from 12 to 30 feet high. Olive trees are extremely hardy, often living 100 years. They tend to take over the immediate area they grow in because of their size. Smooth-margined, gray-green olive leaves are oval and come to a point. They grow 1 to 3 inches long and are paler underneath than above. Their small, inconspicuous, white, 5-petaled flowers have yellow centers and grow in clusters. By autumn, immature green or red olives have become black and shiny and about the size of oval gumballs.

Facts: Drought-tolerant olive trees grow best in full sun, in areas with lots of warm weather and just a bit of a chill. They are not native to the Southwest but were imported from the Mediter-ranean area, where the climate is similar. Olives need to be cured before they can be eaten, otherwise they are extremely bitter. Olive oil is not only tasty, but it is also healthy. No matter how cholesterol-conscious a health advocate is, almost all seem to agree that olive oil, flaxseed oil, and certain fish oils are actually good for your health. Olives are high in vitamin E and reportedly helpful in lowering cholesterol. In Italy and other Mediterranean countries, people cook almost exclusively with olive oil, even dip-ping their bread in it instead of using butter or margarine. After an olive tree has been growing for at least 2 years, you can begin harvesting the fruit.

FOODS
Raw: Before olives can be eaten, they need to be cured. There are several basic methods: most use lye, but some rely on salt. Meth-ods using salt, such as the recipe below, are preferable, since lye is both caustic and unhealthy. Olives are tasty added to all sorts of salads, including taco, potato, and pasta. Cream cheese and olives

make a good sandwich combination, and, of course, olives are delicious plain as a snack.

Cooked: Olives can be cooked with many different foods to make them more flavorful. They are especially good in Mexican dishes such as tamale pie, enchiladas, and nachos.

REAL ITALIAN OLIVES
This recipe was given to me by Assante Borde, who learned it from her father, a native of Veneto, Italy.
Makes about 1 gallon

5-gallon clean plastic bucket	Water
1 gallon firm, ripe, unblemished olives	Large plate, just small enough to fit in the bucket
Kosher salt	

Rinse the olives and make a small lengthwise slit in the side of each one. Put them in the bucket. Add a handful of salt. Then add water to cover and place the plate on top of the floating olives. Every day gently drain the bucket and put in new salt and water. Continue this routine for a month, until the olives are no longer bitter. Remove any mushy olives; they were probably overripe when picked. At the end of the month, rinse off the olives and heat them in the oven at 200 degrees, one layer at a time, turning them once, until they are slightly shriveled. Store them in an airtight container in the refrigerator. No liquid is necessary. They should keep for about a month. If they are too salty, soak them for a few minutes in a little water. If you like plumper olives, do not dry them in the oven, but do store them in water. Some people like to add lemon slices or olive oil to the water. Dried olives last longer, but the others are more succulent and appealing.

PADRES SHOOTING STAR

Dodecatheon clevelandii

Few-Flowered Shooting Star

Features: Padres shooting stars are small, slender perennials with thread-like stems. Growing 4 to 24 inches tall, they are shorter than the surrounding grasses and easy to miss, even after their unique flowers bloom early in spring. Padres shooting star flowers appear to be inside out. They look like someone took a blow-dryer and blew on them until the petals became inverted, much like what happens to umbrellas on a windy day. Initially, the 5 petals, ranging in hue from white to pale lavender, are in a traditional forward-facing position, but as they mature, they creep slowly backward until they resemble the tail of a comet. The small, dark, reddish-brown beak of the flower is in the position of the comet with the petals as its tail. An attractive ring of yellow surrounds this beak. Yellow-green leaves cluster in a rosette around the base of the slightly branched flower stem. However, as the stalk grows, the leaves begin to dry up and disappear. Be careful not to uproot these plants when they are blooming—they are storing up energy in their roots for the coming year.

Facts: There are about 10 western species of shooting star with reddish-lavender flowers. Other varieties grow all over the United States as far north as Alaska. Shooting stars favor moist, grassy environments. In *Wildflowers Across America*, Lady Bird Johnson and Carlton B. Lees mention that one of the plants covered in John Bannister's *Historia Plantarum*, the first book cataloging American plants, printed in 1688, was a Virginian shooting star. In 1678, when Bannister began his research, there were others also "discovering" the New World's flora, which caused some confusion because the same plant discovered by various people was often given more than one name. Since this was also the period when padres were building missions in California, I like to think that padres shooting star was named after some botanically minded padre. Young leaves are available for picking from spring through summer and appear earlier in warmer locales, such as southern California.

FOODS

Tea: Put 2 tablespoons of leaves or a combination of leaves and flowers in a cup. Add boiling water, cover, and steep 5 minutes for a mild and pleasant tea.

Raw: The fresh leaves can be added to salads and sandwiches. They are larger and more tender if you pick them in early spring before the flower stalk appears.

Cooked: The fresh leaves can be steamed, boiled, or roasted but are a bit strong flavored. The tiny roots can also be boiled or roasted, but it is a shame to kill these charming plants in order to obtain such an unsubstantial amount of food.

WILD GREEN SALAD
Serves 2

> 2 cups mild wild greens (such as miner's lettuce,
>   lamb's quarters, amaranth, or sow thistle), chopped
> ¼ cup padres shooting star greens, chopped
> 1 scallion, diced
> 2 tablespoons cheddar cheese, grated
> 1–2 tablespoons ranch dressing

Mix all the ingredients together and serve with fruit and bread.

PALO VERDE

Parkinsonia aculeata

Mexican Palo Verde, Jerusalem Thorn

Features: Up to 30 feet high, but usually much shorter, the beautiful palo verde tree has a softly rounded, almost filmy profile. A profusion of long, graceful, weeping willow-like bipinnate leaves hang down all the way to the ground, with glimpses of sky peeking out through the leaflets. These numerous, exceedingly small, pointed leaflets grow along flexible green leaf stems in winter after sufficient rain has fallen. When the soil dries out in late spring, they drop off. This does not leave much time for photosynthesis, which usually occurs in leaves. Fortunately, 40 percent of palo verde's annual photosynthesis occurs in the green bark along its trunk and branches. In spring, short auxiliary clusters of papery, 5-petaled, yellow flowers appear. Many of them have a single petal which is a rich rusty-orange instead of yellow. They begin to bloom in March at lower elevations, but some of the flowers may linger through August. At higher elevations, they bloom a little later in the season. During summer, the flowers are joined by slender, thin, reddish seedpods of various lengths, which contain both white and brown seeds when mature.

Facts: Palo verde can be found growing along washes in southern California, Arizona, the Colorado Desert, Sonora, Mexico, and tropical America. Because these trees grow in environments which do not have many food sources, they are important to have around. Although the seedpods appear paper thin, they contain several small, succulent seeds. When they are young and tender, these tiny seeds are delicious raw and taste just like fresh peas. Native Americans used the seeds when they were older and drier, grinding them into meal which they cooked as gruel or hot cereal. Cahuillas made mush and cakes from the ground seeds. There are records of many people using the seeds for food during times of famine, and people in Mexico still eat the entire seedpod.

FOODS

Tea: Put a few table-spoons of fresh, cleaned seedpods in a mug. Add boiling water, cover, and steep 5 minutes for a pleasant tea.

Raw: Young palo verde seeds are sweet and taste good raw. They can be gathered in summer.

Cooked: Young, flexible seedpods which are boiled for 20 minutes taste delicious, like sweet peas, and can be eaten as a vegetable.

Dried: After the seedpods have dried, they can be crushed and the seeds removed. The seeds can then be ground and used for hot cereal or combined with other grains and made into a sort of cake.

PALO VERDE SYRUP

Courtesy of Larry Palomera
Makes about 2 cups

1 cup water	1 cup young palo verde seedpods
3–4 sprigs mint	A few drops lemon juice
⅓ cup brown sugar	

Boil all the ingredients together for 2 to 3 minutes. Eat as a dessert. Palo verde syrup makes you burp and is known in Mexico as an aid for gassy stomachs.

PEPPERGRASS

Lepidium nitidum

Features: A small annual plant, peppergrass has stiff, woody, thread-like stems and branches. Most plants are only about 6 to 12 inches tall, but under optimal conditions some varieties can grow almost 36 inches high. Peppergrass appears very fragile, with slender stems and small leaves. Most of the leaves grow at the base, but a few smaller, narrow, pointed leaves grow sparsely scattered along the stem and branches. In spring, inconspicuous white flowers cluster together at the tips of the branches. Small oval, green, paper-like seedpods protrude outward on individual stems, along the stalk and branches. Flowers and seeds can be found growing concurrently on peppergrass, although the seeds remain longer than the flowers, often lasting into summer. As autumn approaches, stems, branches, and seedpods frequently begin to turn a warm red. It is common for people to confuse peppergrass with shepherd's purse, *Capsella bursa-pastoris*. They are both small, very similar in appearance, and are found in the same habitats. However, peppergrass is larger and bushier, while shepherd's purse has more distinctive, more deeply lobed basal leaves. The most obvious difference is their seedpods. Peppergrass seedpods are oval, whereas shepherd's purse seedpods are distinctly heart-shaped. In addition, shepherd's purse usually appears earlier in spring than peppergrass. Although peppergrass can be confused with shepherd's purse, fortunately both plants are edible.

Facts: After winter rains, different varieties of peppergrass can be spotted springing up in both dry, sandy soil and grassy areas as far south as California and north to Alaska and the Yukon. Even though only shepherd's purse produces a tea which is used to stop internal bleeding, peppergrass also has medicinal uses. To cure indigestion, some people drink 1 tablespoon of peppergrass mixed with water, and follow it the next day with a laxative. Peppergrass leaves can be boiled until the water turns brown, then the water used as a hair treatment to clean the scalp and prevent baldness.

Mexicans use the seeds for poultices, whereas Native Americans used them for food. Peppergrass seeds were gathered, parched, ground into a flour, and made into mush.

FOODS

Raw: The seeds are peppery and can be used as a seasoning. Young basal leaves can be added to salads.

Cooked: Spring leaves and plant tops can be boiled and eaten. If they are bitter, boil them in 2 or 3 changes of water. Because of their mustard-like flavor, they are more of a condiment than a potherb.

GAZPACHO WITH PEPPERGRASS
Serves 4–5

1 tablespoon olive oil
2 cloves garlic, minced
½ onion, chopped
6 tomatoes, diced
2 stalks celery, chopped
1 small zucchini, sliced
4 cups water
¼ cup cilantro, chopped
3 sweet basil leaves, chopped
1 teaspoon dried oregano
3 stalks peppergrass, cleaned and chopped
Salt and cayenne pepper
¼ cup fresh lemon juice

Heat the olive oil in a large pot. Then sauté the garlic and onion until clear. Stir in the tomatoes and continue heating over a moderate temperature for 5 minutes. Then add the celery and zucchini. Cover and cook for 5 minutes more. Add all the rest of the ingredients except the lemon juice. Cover and simmer for 10 minutes. Add the lemon juice and serve hot or cold. Garnish each serving with a sprig of cilantro.

PIÑON

Pinus edulis

Features: Piñons are short, spreading, evergreen pine trees which usually grow from 16 to 48 feet high. Their trunks are often divided, and they have many curved and twisted branches. Some of these branches appear to be jutting out almost horizontally, giving the piñon a much broader silhouette than the average pine. Piñons resemble the lovely pine trees so often depicted in Oriental art. Their pinecones are also shorter and squatter than most other pinecones. Exceptionally long, ridged piñon needles grow in bundles of 2 to 5, or singly, and make excellent basket material. New bark appears silvery, but older bark is darker and segmented. Pine nuts are large and easy to gather after the pinecones mature. Piñons do not produce pine nuts until they are 2 years old. After the initial crop, it takes 2 years for new pine nuts to mature. They say that every 7 years there is a bumper crop of pine nuts. In a good year the harvest is incredible, and the ground is literally carpeted with nuts that fall out of the pinecones faster than the animals can eat them.

Facts: Piñons grow scattered throughout the Southwest in piñon-juniper woodlands and dry, rocky places at elevations between 4,000 and 7,500 feet. They are especially evident in Utah, Nevada, California, Arizona, and New Mexico, and can be found growing as far north as Idaho and as far south as Baja, California. Pine nuts are rich in protein and were an important food source for Native Americans. In order to beat the animals

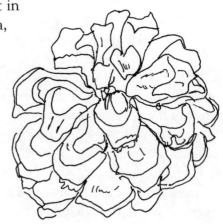

to the pine nuts, they gathered the pinecones before the nuts fell out. After the pinecones were heated over a fire, the pine nuts fell out, and they were then shelled, pounded, and made into gruel, a drink, or cakes to be stored for future use. Sometimes they were mashed, shells and all. Pine nuts are so nutritious and easy to digest that they were even used as baby food. Navajos at Shiprock, New Mexico, heat the piñon pitch, cool it slightly, and put it on slow-healing sores for 2 days in order to draw out poisons. Pine nuts can be gathered from late summer through autumn. If you wish to gather them on Indian reservations or park land, be sure to ask permission.

FOODS

Tea: All pine needles can be brewed into tangy, vitamin C-rich tea. Place a few young needles in a cup, add boiling water, cover, and steep for 5 to 10 minutes, depending on how strong you want it.

Raw: Pine nuts are not only edible but taste very good. Some people find them sweet. If you first heat them for a few minutes in an oven or over a fire, they are easier to shell. Pine nuts make a great snack, and they can be added to cereals, trail mixes, and salads.

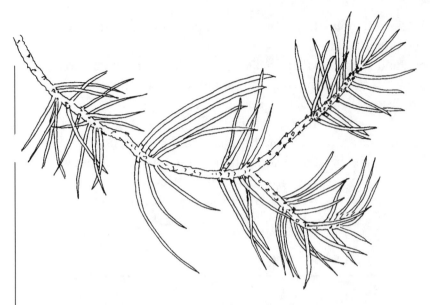

Cooked: Some people prefer to roast pine nuts before eating them. They like the roasted flavor, and the nuts keep longer. Young growth and young, pollen-filled pinecones are also edible. The inner bark, or cambium layer, of all pines is edible, but should only be eaten in an emergency since its removal causes serious, if not fatal, damage to the tree. Pine nuts can be roasted and ground to make a Navajo-style nut butter.

PRESTO PESTO
Serves 4–6

1 pound pasta	2 cups fresh basil, loosely packed
⅓ cup olive oil	½ cup Parmesan cheese
4 cloves garlic	3 tablespoons hot water
¼ cup pine nuts	½ teaspoon salt

Cook the pasta in boiling water until tender. Meanwhile, combine the other ingredients in a blender. Drain the pasta and mix in the pesto. Serve hot or cold with a fresh green salad and hot, crusty bread.

Piñon Pilaf
Serves 4

2 tablespoons butter
1 onion, chopped
⅓ cup pine nuts
1 cup white basmati rice
    or cracked wheat

2 cups broth or water
½ cup raisins
Salt
1 tablespoon butter—
    if using water

Melt the 2 tablespoons butter in a skillet. Sauté the onion until clear. Sauté the pine nuts, then stir in the rice or cracked wheat. Add the broth or water and the raisins. Cover and cook until the mixture begins to boil. Boil gently for 5 minutes and then turn off the heat. Do not disturb for 5 to 10 minutes or until all the liquid is absorbed. Season to taste with salt, and add 1 tablespoon butter if using water.

POMEGRANATE

Punica granatum

Features: Pomegranates are spreading, deciduous shrubs or small trees which grow from 12 to 20 feet tall but are usually shorter, especially if they are kept trimmed. Flexible, wand-like, pomegranate branches are covered with small clusters or pairs of crisp, narrow, shiny, green, smooth-margined, leathery leaves which come to a blunt point. New growth of both the leaves and the occasionally spiny branches is sometimes pale orange. The trunk and more mature branches are covered with silver-gray to brownish-gray bark. In spring, luminescent reddish-orange flowers appear, made up of delicate, crinkly, paper-thin petals. Pomegranate flowers appear to go through two different growth stages. Initially they are soft-petaled flowers with numerous yellow-tipped stamens at their center. After the petals fall, there remain 6 stiff, petal-like sepals arranged in a star-like pattern. Located above this star is the developing fruit. Maturing from yellow-green to rich red, a fully grown pomegranate is about the size of an apple. Pomegranates grow singly or in pairs, and inside each fruit are numerous tightly packed, pulp-covered seeds. The star-like pseudo flower remains upside down beneath the fruit until it is ripe.

Facts: A native of North Africa, pomegranate trees grow on mountain slopes in the tropical climate of temperate zones throughout the world. The name "pomegranate," which comes from Latin, means "apple with many seeds." Pomegranates have been eaten and used by diverse nations throughout history. Greeks have a fable about a lovely woman named Persephone who was kidnaped by one of the gods. She became hungry and ate several seeds from a pomegranate. For each seed she ate, she had to spend one month each year underground, and during these months it was winter in the land. Fortunately, she only ate 6 seeds. Pomegranates are also mentioned in the Old Testament, or Tenach. The menorahs of the tabernacle were designed with

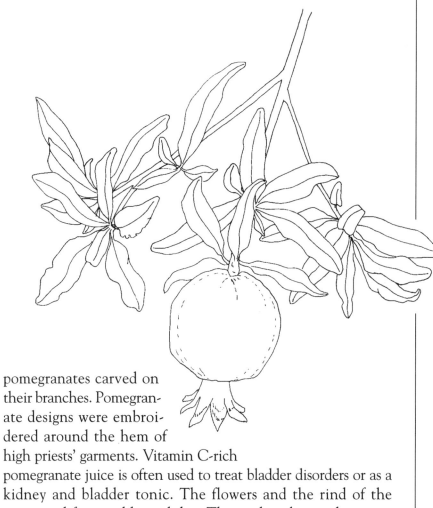

pomegranates carved on their branches. Pomegranate designs were embroidered around the hem of high priests' garments. Vitamin C-rich pomegranate juice is often used to treat bladder disorders or as a kidney and bladder tonic. The flowers and the rind of the unripened fruit yield a red dye. The rind is also used to treat dysentery.

FOODS

Raw: Pomegranates are delicious fresh off the tree or added to fruit salad. However, be careful when eating them because pomegranate juice stains. Quarter the fruit, peel back the leathery rind, and pop the succulent flesh-covered seeds into your mouth. Choice fruit is firm to the touch, has red skin, and the flesh is crimson; brown coloration indicates spoilage.

Cooked: Pomegranates make excellent drinks, syrups, and jellies.

EASY POMEGRANATE JUICE
Makes 1 cup
> 4 pomegranates

Protect your working surface with newspaper. Halve the pome-granates and juice them on an orange juicer. Crush the juice and seed through a strainer. Reserve the juice.

SHORT-CUT GRENADINE SYRUP
Makes 1 cup
> 1 cup pomegranate juice
> 2 tablespoons sugar

Simmer the ingredients together for 10 minutes. Serve hot or cold over pudding, cake, yogurt, or ice cream.

POMEGRANATE PUNCH
Makes 1 quart
> ½ cup grenadine syrup
> 1 quart gingerale
> or
> ¾ cup grenadine syrup
> 3¼ cups lemon/lime soda

Combine either gingerale or lemon/lime soda with the grenadine syrup. Drinks can be garnished with lemon, lime, or orange slices.

POMEGRANATE JELLY
Makes 8 8-ounce jars
> 5 cups pomegranate juice
> 6 cups sugar
> 1 box pectin

Combine the pomegranate juice and sugar in a pot. Heat to a full boil and continue boiling. Stir in the pectin and heat to a rolling boil; continue boiling for 2 to 3 minutes. Pour into canning jars or freezer containers.

REDBERRY

Rhamnus crocea

Spiny Redberry, Buckthorn

Features: Redberry is a low, spreading, evergreen shrub that grows from 3 to 6 feet tall. It has gray-green bark, and its many brittle branches are covered with small leaves and short, slender spines. Its shiny, leathery leaves are elliptical in shape and grow in small bundles along the branches. Even after the tiny white flowers bloom, from March through April, redberry bushes blend into their surroundings. It is only after the small, round, bright red, translucent berries appear during summer that they are noticeable. These berries form in tiny clusters of 2 to several along the branches, with each berry on an individual stem.

Facts: Redberry can be found in chaparral, dry washes, and canyons at elevations below 3,000 feet. It is often confused with holly-leaved coffeeberry, *Rhamnus ilicifolia*, which used to be considered a subspecies of redberry. They are similar; both bushes have white, 4-petaled flowers, but there are noticeable differences. Holly-leaved coffeeberry is a larger plant, with bigger leaves which are sometimes notched. Its berries are about the same size as redberry's, but they are more orange in color. Redberry's leaves are not much larger than its berries, whereas holly-leaved coffeeberry's leaves are significantly larger than its berries. The berries are usually available from late spring into fall.

FOODS

Raw: Redberries can be eaten raw. They are quite juicy but not necessarily sweet or tasty, and they each contain 2 seeds.

Cooked: The berries can probably be cooked into jellies, but they are so small that it would take a lot of time to gather enough.

Pink Cooler
Serves 3
> ¼ cup redberry juice
> 1 tablespoon lemon juice
> 1 cup sugar
> 3 cups water

Mix all the ingredients, chill, and serve.

ROSEMARY

Rosmarinus officinalis

Features: Rosemary is a hardy, perennial native of the Mediterranean area. It is evergreen, drought-tolerant, and covered with attractive needle-like leaves and pale mauve or blue flowers. Because it is easy to grow, requires little maintenance, and is almost impossible to kill, it is very popular throughout the Southwest. A highly aromatic, spreading shrub, rosemary usually grows from 2 to 6 feet tall. Its many flexible, wand-like branches become stiff and woody with age. Needle-like rosemary leaves are dark, glossy green on top, and pale green to almost white underneath. Its small flowers, with 4 irregular petals each, can be found nestled among the leaves which grow in bunches opposite each other along the branches. Under optimal conditions, rosemary bushes begin to blossom as early as February, and the flowers sometimes remain throughout the summer.

Facts: Rosemary requires good drainage, and can be found growing in foothills, chaparral, and drier areas throughout the world. This versatile plant has many medicinal uses. Curiously, its leaves are considered both soothing and invigorating when added to a bath. Shampoo with rosemary is supposed to revitalize your scalp, stimulate new hair growth, and prevent dandruff. Taken internally, this helpful herb is used to aid digestion, especially after eating rich and starchy foods, which is perhaps why it is so often used in sausages. Rosemary is purported to aid memory, and a small amount relieves headaches, although too much may cause one. Rosemary leaves repel moths. In Europe, people combined them with juniper berries and burned them together as a cheap air purifier in hospitals and holy places. These leaves are an antiseptic antioxidant and help preserve food. Although rosemary leaves can be gathered throughout the year, spring leaves are usually fresher and more tender.

FOODS

Tea: Put a few leaves in a mug, fill with boiling water, cover, and steep for 5 minutes. Remove the leaves and serve. Rosemary tea smells and tastes good, and helps to eliminate bad breath.

Raw: The flowers can be eaten raw, and they make a lovely garnish for salads, omelettes, and other dishes.

Cooked: Rosemary is a wonderful seasoning when used in moderation—too much can be overpowering. It is especially good added to Italian food and other tomato-based cuisines. Some gourmet chefs in Albuquerque, New Mexico, like to add rosemary leaves to their breads and biscuits.

ROSEMARY POTATOES

Serves 2

> 4 small red-skinned potatoes
> 1 tablespoon olive oil
> 1 tablespoon
>   rosemary leaves, chopped
> Salt and cayenne pepper
> Paprika

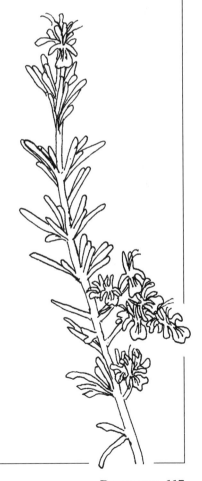

Boil the potatoes for 15 minutes. Remove them from the water and cut them into quarters. Arrange them in an oven-proof dish in a single layer. Sprinkle them with olive oil and rosemary leaves. Season to taste with salt and pepper, then top with paprika. Bake at 350 degrees for ½ hour or until slightly browned. Serve with white vinegar or ketchup.

SALTBUSH

Atriplex lentiformis

Coast Saltbush

Features: There are over 100 species of perennial or annual herbaceous or shrubby saltbushes. Although there is great diversity among the different *Atriplex* species, ranging from the tender-leaved orach, *A. patula*, to the brittle, holly-leaved, fourwing saltbush, *A. canescens*, at one time or another most of them have been dubbed "saltbush." This can be very confusing. The species of saltbush featured in this book is *A. lentiformis*, which is a wide, 3- to 10-foot-high, much-branched bush that manages to prosper despite a shortage of water in its desert habitat. It is covered with an abundance of smooth-margined, pale green, oval leaves which appear whitish and mealy because they are covered with minute white granules. Short flower stems grow at the base of some of the larger leaves. Small leaves grow along their sides, and auxiliary clusters or small spikes of tiny green flowers grow at their tips. The flowers, which bloom from July to November, are followed by equally tiny green seeds. Although the new growth is smooth, flexible, and yellow-green, it becomes rough and darker with age.

Facts: *A. lentiformis* grows throughout the West, as does the more abundant fourwing saltbush. Like most saltbushes, it can be found in arid, alkaline, and saline soils, mostly in desert environments. Saltbushes are very useful plants and are used more often as medicine than food. I was informed by some Hopis at Second Mesa in Arizona that eating too much saltbush at one time is not good for you. They still make a tea from saltbush to relieve flu-related nausea and vomiting and to reduce fevers. The ashes from fourwing saltbush can be used as a leavening agent, and they are one source of piki bread's attractive bluish-green color. Some Native Americans made poultices from saltbush roots, stems, and flowers for use on insect bites. Zunis ground the roots and flowers together, and moistened the mixture with saliva. Moreover, other Indians crushed the flowers and mixed them with water to use as hand soap or to put on ant bites.

Leaves are always best when gathered in spring, and the seeds are not available until late fall or early winter.

Warning: Use saltbush in moderation. Eating too much at one time is not good for you.

FOODS

Raw: The leaves and young shoots can be eaten raw but taste better cooked. Saltbush seeds can be ground into meal and mixed with water to make a pleasant, slightly salty drink.

Cooked: Crushed seeds can be cooked as a cereal or combined with other meals and used for flour. Leaves and young shoots can be cooked as a potherb and are especially good when boiled with meat. Remember that they are salty, and taste your food before seasoning it.

Dried: Saltbush leaves can be dried, powdered, and added to other "flours" to make breads and cakes.

STIR-FRIED SALTBUSH
Serves 2
2 teaspoons butter
2 cloves garlic, minced and chopped
½ onion, chopped
¼ cup saltbush leaves,
    cleaned and chopped
2 cups mild greens, cleaned and chopped
    (see Plant Substitution Appendix)
¼ cup water

Melt the butter and sauté the garlic and onion until clear. Stir in the saltbush leaves and greens, then add the water. Cover and simmer for 4 or 5 minutes. Taste and season if necessary.

SEA ROCKET

Cakile edentula

Beach Rocket

Features: Sea rocket is a fleshy, prostrate, pale green, annual succulent. The stems grow up to 2 feet long but appear much longer. Sea rocket covers the ground like a bumpy carpet, and it's hard to tell where one sprawling plant ends and the next begins. Its wedge-shaped leaves are deeply divided and grow from 1½ to 3 inches long. Although sea rocket has many branches, it keeps a low profile except when it is climbing up or over some local impediment. Its 4-petaled, pink flowers resemble the cruciferous flowers of mustard, *Brassica nigra*, and wild radish, *Raphanus sativus*, both of which are tall, upright plants. They are about the size of wild radish flowers and taste a lot like pungent mustard flowers. Sea rocket blooms from March to October. The fruits are slender seedpods which grow stiffly on individual stems along the branches.

Facts: Sea rocket grows along the West Coast on sandy beaches from San Diego to British Columbia, usually where there is partial shade, whereas wild mustard and wild radish grow inland in open fields and chaparral. In Latin *"edentula"* means "to eat," and *"maritima,"* the name of another species of *Cakile*, means "of the sea." Both names indicate that this is one of several edible seaside plants. Much like mustard, sea rocket tends to have a strong, bitter flavor, even when young. For this reason it is better to use it as a seasoning than as a potherb. Different parts of sea rocket can be eaten during various seasons. The leaves are tender from spring until early summer. Over summer flower buds and young seedpods can be gathered, but late summer is the time to harvest the seeds.

FOODS
Raw: Sea rocket leaves and shoots can be added to salads in moderation.

Cooked: Leaves and shoots can be boiled like spinach and added to quiches, omelettes, soups, casseroles, stir-fries, and stuffing for fish or poultry. Young plants collected from spring to early summer taste best, but even older ones can be used for their peppery, horseradish-like flavor. Flower buds and immature seedpods can also be cooked and used as a flavoring.

Dried: The roots can be dried, ground, and used as a flour extender.

CREAM OF SEA ROCKET SOUP
Serves 2

1 tablespoon butter	1 tablespoon sea rocket leaves,
1 clove garlic, minced	cleaned and chopped
½ onion, chopped	1 cup milk
½ teaspoon thyme	Salt and cayenne pepper
1 potato, diced	Sour cream (optional)
1 cup water	

Melt the butter in a frying pan. Sauté the garlic and onion until clear. Sprinkle with thyme and stir. Add the potato, water, and sea rocket leaves. Bring to a boil. Cover and turn down the heat. Simmer for 15 minutes. Then add the milk and heat but do not boil. Season to taste with salt and pepper and serve garnished with a generous dollop of sour cream, if desired.

SHEEP SORREL

Rumex acetosella

Red Sorrel, Sour Grass

Features: Sheep sorrel is an 8- to 12-inch-tall perennial herb which usually grows in the mountains. Young plants have a basal rosette of narrow leaves shaped like elongated arrowheads. Slightly branched, slender flower stalks spring up in June and July. Each flower stalk and branch is crowned with nodding panicles of inconspicuous yellowish flowers which are followed by tiny seeds encased in paper-like sacs. Sheep sorrel flowers, stalks, and leaves often turn red in autumn. Both the basal rosette of leaves and the flower stalk are joined together at a single rootstock below ground level. Docks and sorrels are often confused for several reasons. They resemble each other in appearance and taste and have similar medicinal uses. Generally, they are divided by size. Dock-like plants under 12 inches tall are considered sorrels, and those over 12 inches tall are considered docks.

Facts: Sheep sorrel grows in exposed fields, waste places, neglected gardens, woods, and along roadsides and the edges of moist lawns. It is widespread throughout North America and can be found in other countries such as France and India. Both docks and sorrels are well known as food plants worldwide. Their young, tender, spring leaves taste best, adding a tangy, lemony flavor to otherwise bland dishes. Sometimes there is a second crop of sorrel in the fall if weather conditions are favorable. Sheep sorrel is high in vitamins A, B complex, C, D, E, and K, as well as calcium, iron, magnesium, silicon, sulphur, and chlorine. It also contains a trace of iodine and zinc and is rich in carotenoids and chlorophyll. Consequently, it is not surprising that this treasure trove of nutrition is said to have a purifying effect on the whole system. Some people use dock seeds as a substitute for tobacco or as part of a tobacco blend. Native Americans gathered the ripe seeds, ground them, and made mush from the resulting meal.

Warning: Sheep sorrel contains oxalic acid and should be eaten in moderation (see Canaigre, page 22).

FOODS

Raw: Young leaves collected in spring are a welcome addition to salads, sandwiches, cottage cheese, and vegetable juices.

Cooked: Sheep sorrel leaves, which are smaller and more tender than most of the other sorrels and docks, taste like spinach with lemon juice added. Leaves are always best when picked in spring before flower stalks appear. They can be boiled, steamed, or sautéed as a vegetable. In addition, several sources suggest using the liquid from boiled sheep sorrel leaves as a rennet substitute because they cause milk to congeal like pudding.

Dried: Leaves can be dried, powdered, stored, and used later as a lemony seasoning.

SOUR SOUP
Serves 2

1 tablespoon butter	1 cup milk
1 clove garlic, minced	1 teaspoon fresh basil,
1 onion, chopped	chopped
1 cup water	Salt and cayenne pepper
1 tablespoon sheep sorrel	Parmesan cheese
leaves, cleaned and chopped	

Melt the butter and sauté the garlic and onion until clear. Add the water and bring to a boil. Add the sheep sorrel, cover, and simmer for 5 minutes. Then add the milk and basil. Continue heating for 5 more minutes, but do not boil. Season to taste with salt and pepper. Serve with Parmesan cheese and hot, crusty pumpernickel bread.

SPEARMINT

Mentha spicata

Features: Slightly branched spearmint is a 2- to 4-foot-tall, square-stemmed perennial mint that spreads rapidly via a creeping rootstock from which large colonies of new plants arise. It has pairs of leaves opposite each other along stems and branches. The bright green, slightly hairy leaves each grow on a small individual leaf stem or are directly attached to the plant. Spearmint leaves are spear-shaped with serrated margins. White to lavender flowers grow in whorled clusters arranged in tiers above the terminal pairs of leaves. They usually bloom from late summer through fall. Both leaves and stems sometimes become purplish towards autumn. Because mints hybridize freely, it is not always easy to distinguish one species from another.

Facts: Aromatic spearmint grows in or near water where there is partial shade at elevations under 5,000 feet throughout the United States and in other countries. Not only is spearmint delicious and refreshing, but it is also good for you.

The leaves are high in vitamins A, C, and K, calcium, and manganese. Peppermint, *Mentha piperita*, and spearmint have similar medicinal properties. Both can be brewed into teas which soothe frayed nerves, upset stomachs, colic, heartburn, gas pains, and nervous headaches. Steam from boiled mint leaves can be inhaled to clear sinuses. Mint tea is so calming that it can even help induce sleep. Hopis and Navajos used mint leaves to flavor cornmeal mush. Spearmint smells good to people but apparently not to insects. Black flies, beetles, cabbage beetles, butterfly caterpillars, ants, fleas, and sometimes aphids are repelled by it. When gathering spearmint from May to September, it is possible to collect some without harming the plants. If you just remove some of the leaves, or even the tip of a branch, but leave the roots and part of the plant intact, it will continue to grow and propagate.

FOODS

Tea: Pour 1 cup of boiling water over ½ cup fresh spearmint leaves or 1 tablespoonful dried. Cover and steep for 10 minutes. Drink as is or sweeten with sugar or honey. Mint combines well with other teas.

Raw: The leaves taste great right off the plant. If you are hiking, you might want to add a leaf to your canteen for a refreshing change from plain water. Mint leaves are also very good added to salads, and many Middle Eastern recipes call for them.

Cooked: Mint jelly is tasty and often accompanies meat or turkey. Although this jelly has a nice minty flavor, it does not have the bright green color we generally associate with mint leaves, so most mint jelly recipes call for food coloring.

GREEK SALAD

Serves 4

Salad:

    2 cups romaine lettuce,
      chopped
    1 green pepper, cut in strips
    1 red pepper, cut in strips
    1 cucumber, skinned and cubed
    1 tablespoon fresh mint,
      chopped
    4 tomatoes, cubed
    ½ red onion, minced
    8 ounces feta cheese,
      crumbled
    Black olives
      (optional)

Dressing:

    2 tablespoons olive oil
    2 tablespoons lemon juice
    2 cloves garlic, crushed

Combine all the ingredients
except the feta cheese
and olives. Mix with the
dressing. Top with feta
cheese and sprinkle with
olives. Traditionally,
Greek salad is served
with pita bread.

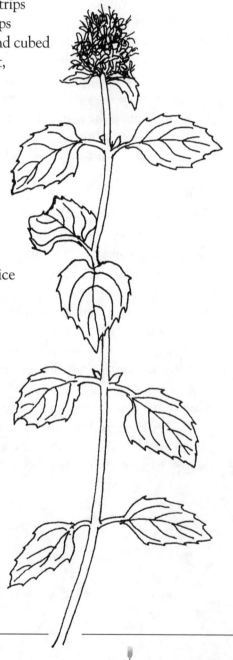

REFRESHING YOGURT SALAD

Serves 4

    1 cup yogurt
    2 cucumbers,
        skinned and grated
    1 clove garlic, crushed
    2 tablespoons fresh lemon juice
    ½ teaspoon dried
        mint leaves, crumbled
    ½ teaspoon dried
        dill, crumbled
    ¼ cup onion, minced
    Salt (optional)

Combine all the ingredients. This salad makes a tasty dip for pita bread and a good condiment for falafels.

STICKY CINQUEFOIL

Potentilla glandulosa

Features: At first glance, perennial sticky cinquefoil, which grows from 1 to 3 feet tall, looks like a strawberry plant that did not know when to stop growing. Its leaves, with their small, oval leaflets and serrated margins, look just like strawberry leaves. But strawberry leaves have only 3 leaflets each, whereas sticky cinquefoil may have young leaves of 3 leaflets, but mature leaves are only topped with 3 leaflets and have 2 to 3 pairs of leaflets continuing down their spines. Both plants have small, 5-petaled, white flowers which bloom in spring, and both are covered with delicate white hairs. As its name implies, sticky cinquefoil is slightly sticky to the touch. It usually blooms from April to June.

Facts: Over 250 species of *Potentilla* grow in the Northern Hemisphere; most can be found growing in damp or wet, shady hillside locations. Sticky cinquefoil grows below 2,000 feet. Its generic name, *Potentilla*, refers to its potent nature. Its common name, cinquefoil, comes from two French words, *cinq*, which is the number five, and *foil*, which means leaf. Native Americans thought highly of sticky cinquefoil roots as a food source. In addition to being edible, sticky cinquefoil has medicinal uses. Tea brewed from its leaves can be used as a gargle or mouthwash, as well as utilized to relieve diarrhea and to control fevers. Sticky cinquefoil leaves were made into poultices and applied to skin wounds. A different tea, brewed from the entire plant or only the roots, was drunk to cure stomach cramps or made into a soothing, astringent lotion. The leaves, worn in shoes while hiking, are supposed to prevent blisters.

FOODS

Tea: For a spring tonic, put 6 young leaves in a mug, fill with boiling water, cover, and steep for 10 minutes. Remove the leaves. Drink the resulting tea in moderation; remember, this tea is a cure for diarrhea. Sticky cinquefoil leaves also can be used to brew a pleasantly mild sun tea.

Raw: The roots can be eaten raw and are a good source of carbohydrates. Collect them in early spring or late autumn.

Cooked: The roots can be baked, boiled, or roasted like potatoes, although they are much smaller.

SUNFLOWER

Helianthus annuus

Common Sunflower

Features: It is hard to miss beautiful, golden-yellow sunflowers in the fields, especially since some varieties grow up to 20 feet tall, with a flower head over 1 foot in diameter. There are 67 varieties of sunflower. Although they may be annual or perennial, branched or unbranched, all are coarse with simple oval or heart-shaped leaves which grow opposite or alternately along stout, rough stalks. In spring, showy sunflower heads are made up of centers filled with yellow, brown, or purplish-brown disk flowers surrounded by a halo of yellow ray flowers. Behind the ray flowers are stiff, ray-like sepals which remain even after the ray flowers wither and drop off. In summer, the disk flowers are replaced by large, edible seeds arranged in attractive, geometric patterns.

Facts: These impressive flowers are native to the Americas. Cultivated by Hopis and other Native Americans, they were "discovered" by the Spanish, introduced to Europe, exported to Russia, and brought back to the United States. Often the unwitting gift of a passing bird, they grow in dry, disturbed waste places and open ground in temperate zones throughout the West and worldwide at elevations below 5,000 feet. All parts of the sunflower are usable. Sunflower seeds are one of the most important sources of oil in the world. Purple and black dyes can be made from these seeds, and yellow dye from the flowers. Roasted seeds and seed shells can be brewed into a coffee substitute. Fiber can be made from sunflower stalks, and the leaves can be dried and smoked. Native Americans parched the seeds, ground them, and used the meal for bread or cakes. A tea made from the dried plant was added to bathwater to provide relief from arthritic pain and swollen joints. In addition, sunflowers can absorb water from the soil, and have been used in the Netherlands to reclaim marshy ground.

FOODS

Raw: The disk flowers can be eaten raw. The seeds make a great snack and a tasty addition to salads, cereals, and trail mix. They can also be used for sprouting.

Cooked: Entire young flowerheads can be boiled and eaten or added to breads. The buds can be steamed. The roots are also edible but do not produce tubers like Jerusalem artichokes.

DAD'S MUESLI
Makes 8½ cups

4 cups steel cut oats
1 cup sunflower seeds,
  shelled
1 cup dried figs, chopped
½ cup dried peaches,
  chopped

½ cup dried apricots,
  chopped
½ cup raisins
½ cup date pieces
½ cup walnuts, chopped

Mix all the ingredients and store in the refrigerator. In the morning, moisten your serving with milk and let it stand for ½ hour before eating, or heat it slightly, adding more liquid if necessary. For a special treat, add a grated apple just before serving.

TRAIL MIX
Makes 6¼ cups

1 cup almonds
1 cup walnuts, chopped
2 cups sunflower seeds, shelled
¾ cup raisins
¾ cup date bits
¾ cup carob chips

Mix all the ingredients together and store for future use.

TANSY MUSTARD

Descurainia spp.

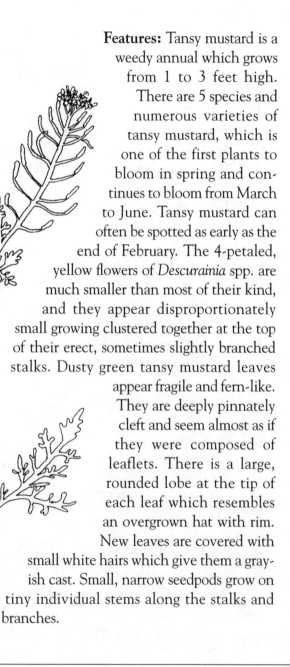

Features: Tansy mustard is a weedy annual which grows from 1 to 3 feet high. There are 5 species and numerous varieties of tansy mustard, which is one of the first plants to bloom in spring and continues to bloom from March to June. Tansy mustard can often be spotted as early as the end of February. The 4-petaled, yellow flowers of *Descurainia* spp. are much smaller than most of their kind, and they appear disproportionately small growing clustered together at the top of their erect, sometimes slightly branched stalks. Dusty green tansy mustard leaves appear fragile and fern-like. They are deeply pinnately cleft and seem almost as if they were composed of leaflets. There is a large, rounded lobe at the tip of each leaf which resembles an overgrown hat with rim. New leaves are covered with small white hairs which give them a grayish cast. Small, narrow seedpods grow on tiny individual stems along the stalks and branches.

Facts: Tansy mustard grows in dry, open or wooded areas throughout the West. All species are edible, although due to their peppery flavor tansy mustard seeds are often considered more a spice than a food. Nevertheless, Native Americans collected the seeds, parched and ground them, and made soup or combined the resulting meal with other meals to make mush. They also gathered new leaves before the flowers appeared, boiled or roasted them between hot rocks, and ate them. Unmixed mustard flour was used for poultices or brewed into a medicinal tea which was drunk during summer. Mexicans use mustard poultices on wounds. Pottery paint was prepared from these seeds. They were ground on a mortar until they became an oily liquid; then ground-up iron was added.

FOODS

Cooked: Young leaves can be boiled but may require several changes of water if they are bitter. The seeds can be parched, roasted in an oven, ground, and used as a spicy condiment or eaten as an ingredient in mush. Remember that they are mustard seeds and should be used sparingly.

TOMATILLO

Physalis pruinosa

Features: Tomatillos are hairy, spreading plants, most of which are annual. Usually growing from 6 to 24 inches high, tomatillos have grainy textured branches and small clusters of shiny green leaves. The leaves are basically oval in shape with shallow, irregular lobes. Each leaf grows on an individual stem. The flowers and fruit are really special. Nodding tomatillo flowers, which bloom from spring into summer, appear to consist of a single, 5-angled, ruffled petal. They range in color from white to yellow and are bell-shaped, hanging suspended from the branches either singly or in small clusters of 2 to 5. Each flower has a rich, dark, purple-brown center. Tomatillo fruit is a many-seeded, yellow-green berry about the size of a pea. When it is cut open, it looks like a tiny tomato. Each berry is encased in a thin yellow-green husk which resembles a miniature hanging Chinese paper lantern. All parts of the plant are slightly sticky. Tomatillos are often confused with ground cherries, *Physalis hederaefolia*. As members of the tomato family, both have edible berries and inedible leaves. The most obvious difference between these two plants is their berries. Both grow in husks, but ground cherry berries are orange-rust or red, not green. Ground cherry is also a more vine-like plant, and the unripe fruit of some species is considered poisonous if too many are eaten. Although wolfberry, *Lycium pallidum*, is sometimes called tomatillo, its orange to red berries are smaller than tomatillo berries. It can easily be distinguished from ground cherry by its thorny branches.

Facts: Tomatillos grow in moist to dry sandy soil at altitudes below 8,000 feet scattered throughout the United States. Tomatillo fruit is available in late summer and fall. It's always safest to eat fully ripe tomatillo and ground cherry berries to avoid risking any confusion with poisonous species of ground cherry. If the fruit you pick is not quite ripe, you can complete the ripening process at home by placing the berries in a sunny location like a

south-facing windowsill. Do
not remove the husks
until you are ready to eat
the ripe berries. When
they are left in their
husks, they keep for
weeks. The tastiest ones
are those which are
slightly soft and encased in
bright, healthy-looking husks.

FOODS
Raw: Fully ripe berries can be eaten in the same
manner you would use tomatoes. They are tender,
sweet, and juicy. If the berries are bitter, sour, or
unpleasant, they are not ripe.

Cooked: After being roasted to remove their skins,
tomatillos can be made into sauces, preserves, and relishes or
cooked with scrambled eggs.

TOMATILLO SALSA
This is a family recipe from John Gomez, who is from Cilayona,
Mexico.
Makes about 1 pint

½ pound tomatoes, cubed	3 green onions, chopped
½ pound tomatillos, roasted	1 large handful cilantro,
1 jalapeño pepper	chopped
(remove the seeds	½ teaspoon lime juice
for a milder flavor)	2 teaspoons salt
Cumin (comino) seeds,	
ground (optional)	

Combine all the ingredients in a blender and blend to the desired
consistency. Serve as a dip with tortilla chips or onions, or use as
a delicious condiment with Mexican foods.

TOOTHWORT

Cardamine californica

Milkmaids, Pepperfoot, Dentaria, Wild Horseradish, Pepper Root

Features: Perennial toothwort plants come as a pleasant surprise if you are fortunate enough to spot them growing nestled among the taller, leafier plants of oak woodland and chaparral environments. Young plants appear in early spring, consisting of a single 3-leaflet leaf lying close to the ground. The leaflets are roundish with slightly serrated margins. Slender flower stalks, usually unbranched and growing from 6 to 12 inches high, arise from the base of the initial leaf. On rare occasions, toothwort may grow up to 2 feet tall. Additional trifoliate leaves grow alternately near the base of the flower stalk. These leaves are smaller than the initial one, and each is on its own stem. Toothwort is crowned with small clusters of tiny, white to pale rose, 4-petaled flowers. Toothwort leaves are darker above than underneath. Its rootstocks are relatively thick and fleshy for such a slender plant, and sometimes there are tubers. Toothwort is a relative of horseradish, *Cochlearia armoracia*. Both plants have strong, sharp-flavored roots.

Facts: Toothwort does best in moist, shady locations and can be found along streambanks in mountain and coastal regions of the Pacific Coast states and scattered through the Midwest in wooded or chaparral areas. Its roots can be gathered year-round but should only be collected if absolutely necessary since this can kill the plant. However, if you are careful you can gather some of the root and still save the plant by breaking off small

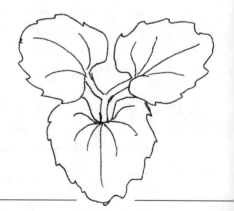

sections of the harvested root and replanting them. Amazingly, they will grow. Although the roots can be gathered at any season, it is safest to gather the roots when the plant blooms in spring so that you can make a positive identification.

FOODS

Raw: The roots can be eaten raw as a snack or added to salads.

Cooked: The roots can be added as a spicy seasoning to cooked foods such as meats, greens, and stir-fries. They can also be boiled, steamed, or stir-fried. The longer you cook the roots, the milder their flavor becomes. Slicing the roots before cooking improves their flavor and texture.

TOOTHWORT DIP

Makes 3 cups
> 2 tablespoons butter
> ½ onion, finely chopped
> ½ cup toothwort root,
>   thinly sliced
> 2 cups sour cream
>   or plain yogurt
> Salt
> Crackers

Melt the butter in a frying pan. Sauté the onion until clear but not brown. Stir in the sliced toothwort root and continue cooking for 5 more minutes, stirring occasionally. Add the cooked onion and toothwort to the sour cream or yogurt. Season to taste with salt and serve with crackers.

WILD HYACINTH

Dichelostemma pulchella

Blue Dicks

Features: Wild hyacinths are perennial, grass-like herbs which grow from 1 to 2 feet tall. By the time wild hyacinths bloom in spring, their stems are almost leafless. Prior to this time there are usually several grass-like leaves which grow up to 10 inches tall. Leaves and flower stalk are joined to an edible, underground corm. Appearing from February through May, the attractive flowerhead is made up of 4 to 10 brilliant purplish-blue flowers clustered together. Wild hyacinth is often confused with brodiaea, *Brodiaea jolonensis*, which grows in a similar range. It is important to recognize the difference since brodiaea is not considered edible. The easiest way to distinguish the two plants is to examine their flowers. Brodiaea's flowers are larger, have fewer per flowerhead, and are more reddish in color.

Facts: Wild hyacinths favor open grassy places, dry arroyos, vacant lots, chaparral, deserts, and coastal sage as far north as Utah and from southern California to southern New Mexico and northern Sonora.

Wild hyacinth's edible corms vary in palatability, but most are tasty and nut-like. Native Americans and early settlers ate them frequently, using digging sticks to gather them. The settlers nicknamed the corms "grassnuts."

For your protection, wait until the plants bloom in early spring before gathering corms in order to make a positive identification of the plant. Only gather where there is an abundance of plants, keeping the larger corms and leaving the smaller ones in the ground to propagate.

FOODS

Raw: The corms are delicious raw. The flowers are edible and make an attractive garnish when added to salads, pastas, and other dishes.

Cooked: The corms can be fried, boiled, or roasted. Because they are so small, they do not require much cooking time; however, Cahuillas used to boil them for ½ hour.

WILD HYACINTH STIR-FRY
Serves 2

    1 tablespoon olive oil
    2 cloves garlic, minced
    ½ onion, sliced
    1 tablespoon grated ginger or 1 teaspoon powdered ginger
    ½ cup wild hyacinth corms, cleaned and sliced
    ½ cup broccoli, chopped
    2 cups mild greens, chopped
      (see Plant Substitution Appendix)
    2 tablespoons soy sauce
    Water

Heat the oil. Sauté the garlic and onion until clear. Stir in the ginger, corms, and broccoli. Cook for 2 to 3 minutes over medium heat. Add the greens, soy sauce, and a little water if necessary. Stir, then cover and continue cooking over low heat until the greens are tender, about 5 minutes.

WILD ONION

Allium spp.

Features: There are over 500 species of allium worldwide. All grow from underground bulbs, have several basal, grass-like leaves, have a terminal flowerhead comprised of many flowers, and have a strong onion scent, which distinguishes them from similar-looking plants. In spring, 1- to 2-foot-high unbranched, hollow stalks of perennial wild onion appear, surrounded by 4 to 6 long slender leaves which grow 6 to 12 inches high. The flowerhead is made up of numerous small 3-petaled flowers, which are usually some shade of purple. By the time the flowerhead is fully mature, the leaves have passed their prime and begun to die back. The easiest way to identify an onion or garlic plant is to smell it. All parts smell like onion. Be sure to smell it before eating it to avoid confusing wild onion with death camas, *Zygadenus venenosus*—which could prove fatal. Their bulbs appear similar, but death camas bulbs have no onion smell. When they are flowering, it is much easier to distinguish between the two plants since death camas has white flowers which are not arranged in a flowerhead. Both plants have grass-like leaves, but wild onion's are basal, whereas those of death camas are both basal and growing along the stalk.

Facts: Wild onions can be found growing throughout the Southwest on either dry slopes or damp ground, depending on the species. Wild onions are never poisonous, but they do add an interesting flavor to the milk of the cows that eat them. The bulbs can be gathered in early spring or fall, and young spring leaves are best. Onions were boiled down to a thick syrup which was used medicinally to alleviate coughs, colds, and throat irritations. Crushed onions were applied to insect bites and stings or used as a preventive before insects had a chance to attack. All species of allium have antibiotic properties. Onions and garlic are high in vitamin C and therefore effective in preventing scurvy. Native Americans used onions to stimulate weak appetites. Currently, pills manufactured from onions are being used to relieve rhinitis and hay fever.

FOODS

Raw: Both the young leaves and bulbs can be eaten raw; however, consumption of them will not go unnoticed by those around you. A few raw onions perk up salads, dips, and sandwiches. My father loved raw onion sandwiches, a taste he acquired from his parents, who came from western Europe.

Cooked: The bulbs can be steamed, grilled, boiled, baked, roasted, or added to other foods—in the same way you would use domestic onions. When roasting onions, they should be left unpeeled until they are cooked, then pierced in order to release the steam before they are eaten.

Dried: Wild onion bulbs can be dried for future use.

Potato Salad
Serves 6–8

> 6 potatoes, boiled and cubed
> 6 wild onion stalks, diced
> ¾ cup sour cream
> 2 tablespoons lemon juice
> Salt and cayenne pepper
> Wild onion blossoms

Mix all the ingredients together except the blossoms. Season to taste with salt and pepper. Garnish with the blossoms.

WILD VIOLET

Viola pedunculata

Johnny-Jump-Up

Features: Small, fragile, yellow-flowering wild violets are only one of over 50 species. They are perennials which grow from 4 to 6 inches high in southern California and bloom from February to April. Each plant is comprised of a few slender flower stalks topped by a single flower and several thread-like leaf stems, each topped by a solitary, shiny green, heart-shaped leaf with shallowly serrated margins. Both stalks and stems are joined atop a single rootstock. The white, pink, pale mauve, rich purple, blue, or yellow violet blossoms of various species have 5 irregular petals. Violets spread by runners, and some species are endangered.

Facts: Wild violet can be found hidden among taller grasses in moist, partially shady woodlands and chaparral areas throughout the United States from California up through northern Alaska, usually at altitudes below 7,000 feet. All parts of violet plants are edible and very nutritious. Two tiny leaves provide a whole day's requirement of vitamin C, and they are instrumental in curing colds and sore throats. Slightly heated violet leaves were placed on bruises, and the fresh leaves were used both internally and externally as a cure for cancer. The flowers, which are rich in vitamins A and C, were utilized by early botanists to cure and prevent bronchial ailments. Napoleon's followers thought so highly of this little flower that they chose it for their symbol. Spring and early summer are the best times to collect plants.

FOODS

Tea: Put 1 tablespoon of fresh leaves or 1 teaspoon of dried leaves in a cup. Add boiling water, cover, and steep for 5 minutes. This tea smells wonderful and tastes pleasant. However, it is slightly laxative, so drink it in moderation.

Raw: The leaves and flowers taste good raw, and can be added to salads and sandwiches or used as a garnish.

Cooked: Sometimes violet flowers are candied to be used as cake decorations. The leaves can be cooked and made into sauces and jellies.

VIOLET OMELETTE
Serves 2

4 eggs	¼ cup wild violet leaves,
2 teaspoons milk	cleaned and chopped
1 tablespoon butter	Salt and cayenne pepper

Beat the eggs and milk together while you are melting the butter. Add the eggs to the butter and heat at a fairly high temperature. Sprinkle the leaves over the moist eggs. When the eggs are browned on one side, flip them over and brown the other. When the second side is lightly browned, season with salt and pepper and serve.

WINTER CRESS

Barbarea orthoceras

Features: Annual winter cress first appears as a basal rosette of smooth, shiny, bright green leaves, sometimes as early as February. These lovely leaves are lyre-shaped and deeply divided, sometimes almost to the midvein, and have large terminal lobes. Later, the slightly branched flower stalk appears, reaching heights of 1 to 2 feet. Smaller leaves that vary in shape grow along the stalks, but they are not as deeply divided as the basal leaves. Small, 4-petaled, mustard-colored flowers grow at the top of the stalk. Later, small, narrow, upright seedpods appear, growing along the stalk on tiny stems. Each seedpod contains many seeds. Winter cress flowers from May to July. The initial rosette of leaves often remains during winter and continues growing under warm, favorable conditions.

Facts: Winter cress grows in rich, moist soil by roadsides and streams from California up to Alaska. Its leaves are high in iron, potassium, phosphorus, calcium, and vitamins A, B, and C. Young leaves should be gathered in early spring before the flower stalk appears. After the flower stalk appears, first flower buds and later immature seedpods can be collected. Mature seedpods can be gathered from late summer until early autumn.

FOODS
Raw: Young leaves and stems can be eaten raw in salads and sandwiches, but they tend to be bitter.

Cooked: Young leaves can be boiled in more than 1 change of water to eliminate bitterness, then used in omelettes and quiches. They can also be fermented like sauerkraut after they have been steamed for 15 to 20 minutes.

WINTER CRESS SOUP
Serves 2

    4 cups homemade chicken broth
    2 teaspoons sweet paprika
    2 potatoes, cubed
    2 tablespoons winter cress leaves, chopped
    Salt and cayenne pepper
    Sour cream

Combine the broth, paprika, and potatoes. Cover and bring to a boil. Lower the heat and simmer for 20 minutes or until the potatoes are cooked. Add the leaves and cook over medium heat for 5 more minutes. Season to taste with salt and pepper, and serve with a dollop of sour cream.

YAMPA

Perideridia spp.

Wild Caraway, Squawroot, Yamp

Features: Yampa is a slender perennial with a slightly branched flower stalk which can reach 4 feet in height but usually is under 2 feet tall. From June to July, umbrella-like compound clusters of small white flowers appear. The flowers are followed by tiny, caraway-like seeds. Yampa has a few grass-like leaves which are narrow and segmented, resembling a lopsided trident. These leaves are usually withered and gone by the time the plant blooms. Thick yampa roots produce small tubers which grow singly or in small clusters. It is important not to confuse yampa with poison hemlock, *Conium maculatum* (see page 220). All species of yampa are edible, whereas poison hemlock is deadly. Although their flowers are similar, there are some major differences between these two plants. Poison hemlock is much taller, has a stouter stem, and the stem usually has purple blotches near its base. Its leaves are more fern-like and less thready, and it smells bad when bruised.

Facts: There are about 8 different species of yampa growing throughout the West, especially in California, Oregon, Idaho, Wyoming, Utah, and Nevada. All varieties except one grow on damp ground with partial shade in meadows, valleys, and on mountain slopes at elevations below 11,000 feet. Yampa roots are sweet and delicious, ranging from nut-like to carrot-like in flavor. They are easy to dry and store well. Native Americans dried them, soaked them in water, ground them into flour, and cooked the flour into mush. Settlers learned about yampa from Native Americans, and it was an important food source for Lewis and Clark. Edible yampa seeds were parched and eaten in mush or used as a seasoning. They were also considered good for treating colds and indigestion. Yampa seed poultices were placed on sore eyes and bruises, and the roots were chewed to relieve sore throats. In Colorado, yampa was such a valued and abundant plant that the local people almost named their state after it. Unfortunately, some species of yampa are now on the rare and endangered list, so please check the list before you harvest any plants.

FOODS
Raw: The crisp tubers are tasty anytime, but May and June are the best times to gather them.

Cooked: The roots can be cooked any way you would prepare potatoes. They can also be boiled to make soup.

Dried: The tubers are easy to dry in the sun and can be eaten as a snack or stored for future use.

CREAMED YAMPA AND VEGETABLES
Serves 4–6

2 cups water	12 ounces pasta
2 cups yampa tubers	2 tablespoons butter
4 small boiling onions,	4 tablespoons flour
quartered	1½ cups milk
1 cup carrots, diced	Salt and cayenne
1 cup peas	pepper

Put the yampa tubers and onions in a pot with the water and heat until boiling. Add the carrots and boil for 5 minutes, then add the peas and cook for 5 minutes more. Meanwhile, add the pasta to a pot of boiling water and cook until tender. Then melt the butter in a large frying pan. Add the flour, stirring constantly to prevent burning. Slowly pour in the milk. Continue stirring until the sauce is smoothly blended. Season to taste with salt and pepper. Drain the vegetables and add them to the cream sauce. Then drain the pasta and serve it swimming in creamed vegetables.

PART II

QUESTIONABLE PLANTS—
RECIPES INCLUDED

COFFEEBERRY

Rhamnus californica

California Coffeeberry, California Buckthorn, Southern California Coffeeberry

Features: Coffeeberry is a small evergreen tree or shrub which grows from 3 to 12 feet tall. Its bright green, oblong leaves have serrated margins and are usually between 1 and 3 inches long. Coffeeberry flowers, which appear in May and June, are small and green. They are followed by copious quantities of green to red berries, which turn an enticing, shiny black when they mature in autumn. But although the berries are seductive, they do not taste as good as they look—in fact they are bitter. Moreover, the plant has laxative properties so if you do eat them be prepared to cope with the results.

Facts: Coffeeberry can be found growing in chaparral, on rocky hillsides, beach dunes, shaded slopes, and in ravines and arroyos at altitudes below 3,500 feet from California to Canada. Although coffeeberry is not the official cascara sagrada, *Rhamnus purshiana*, it also has laxative properties. Cascara sagrada is taller, from 8 to 40 feet in height, and is usually found further north along the Pacific Coast. Native Americans used the bark from both trees as a laxative. First they scored the bark and removed a section. Then the peeled section was dried for a year before it was used. Later a portion was cut off and soaked overnight or boiled for 1 hour before the resulting liquid was administered to the patient. Cahuillas soaked the fresh berries in warm water to produce a milder laxative drink, which was also used as a tonic. In addition, dried bark was ground and used as a powder. A method Native Americans utilized to treat poison oak was to boil cascara sagrada bark with salt, bathe the afflicted area with the liquid, and let it dry, repeating the procedure for 2 to 3 days until the patient was better.

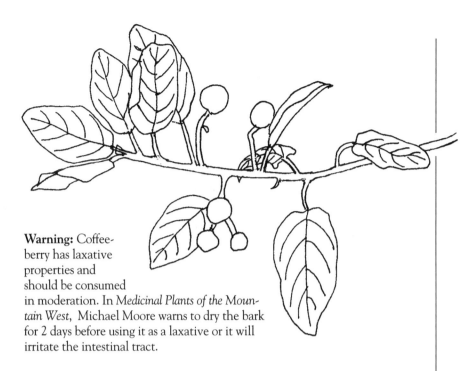

Warning: Coffee-
berry has laxative
properties and
should be consumed
in moderation. In *Medicinal Plants of the Moun-*
tain West, Michael Moore warns to dry the bark
for 2 days before using it as a laxative or it will
irritate the intestinal tract.

FOODS

Raw: The berries can be eaten raw but taste bitter.

Cooked: Some people make a coffee-like beverage from coffeeberry seeds.

DEFINITELY NOT COFFEE

Based on a recipe Christopher Nyerges learned from John
Watkins.

1 gallon firm, ripe coffeeberries

After gathering the berries, let them rot. Next, strain the results
and save the seeds. Wash the seeds and dry them in the oven at a
medium temperature. Then grind them coarsely in a coffee mill.
Roast the resulting grounds at 375 degrees until they turn deep
brown, stirring occasionally to prevent them from burning. Brew
this unusual drink as you would coffee.

COLUMBINE

Aquilegia spp.

Features: Columbines are perennial, bushy plants which have spectacular flowers. Although the flowers are very conspicuous, most of these plants are considerably under 3 feet in height, and they grow nestled among taller plants and shrubs, making them difficult to detect. Columbine flowers, which bloom from spring through summer, are pale mauve, soft red, yellow, white, or pale blue. The tips of their 5 petals point upwards like a jester's hat, and their bases form long, hollow spurs which extend backward. Columbines only have a few leaves, and they attach directly to the stem and occasional branch. The leaves are trifoliate, and most have deeply toothed margins.

Facts: Columbine grows in a variety of moist environments ranging from moist woods and meadows to mountain slopes in northern temperate zones and is widespread in western Canada and most states, including parts of Alaska. Finding a columbine is like finding an unexpected treasure. Although columbines are used medicinally, most parts of the plants contain a cyanogenic glycoside which is poisonous and can prove fatal if consumed in excess. This harmful substance is most concentrated in the roots and seeds, and children have died from consuming the seeds. Young leaves gathered in spring were made into lotions used to relieve sore mouths and throats. Native Americans boiled and ate the young leaves, and in summer they ate the flowers. They also made a tea from the boiled roots in summer to treat diarrhea. The fresh roots, mashed in olive oil, were used externally to relieve painful arthritis. For medicinal purposes, roots and seeds are gathered in summer.

Warning: Do not eat the roots or seeds because they contain poisonous hydrocyanic acid.

FOODS
Raw: The flowers are safe to eat in moderation, and they make a lovely garnish for salads.

EPAZOTE

Chenopodium ambrosioides

Mexican Tea, Pazote, American Wormseed

Features: There are several varieties of epazote. All are typical chenopodiums with much-branched, ridged stems, and alternating, elliptical, pointed, green leaves with irregularly toothed margins. Epazote grows from 2 to 4 feet high and is usually an annual, though occasionally a short-lived perennial. Sometimes the leaves are sparse, but more often they grow in abundance, frequently clustering at the top of the stalk and branches. Older leaves often become tinged with red. In spring, crowded clusters of inconspicuous, tiny, greenish flowers grow at the tips of stalk and branches, followed by minute green seeds. Epazote is distinguished by a strong, unpleasant odor when crushed. It is important to distinguish epazote from the related lamb's quarters, *Chenopodium album*, since lamb's quarters is always edible, and epazote should be eaten in moderation. Some side effects of overindulging in epazote are dizziness, nausea, and vomiting. Epazote's leaves are the same shade of green on both sides, and they are longer, lighter, and more deeply toothed than lamb's quarters leaves. By contrast, the leaves of lamb's quarters are paler underneath than above, sometimes appearing almost white. These two plants can also be distinguished by smell. Epazote smells bad, whereas lamb's quarters has no discernible odor.

Facts: Epazote grows along inland streambeds, salt marshes, and disturbed sites in sandy soil. It is easy to understand why epazote is used more as a condiment than a food. Young spring leaves are most often used as seasoning, and in Mexico they are a very popular ingredient in bean recipes because they reputedly prevent or eliminate gas and aid digestion. Also beans taste better with a little epazote seasoning. Medicinally, epazote tops are soaked in water for several hours, and the resulting liquid is drunk to stop chills. Externally, epazote is considered somewhat antibacterial and effective against infections. The seeds are believed to be a safe vermifuge against roundworms for everyone except pregnant women.

Warning: Too much epazote is harmful to your health, but a moderate amount apparently has no ill effects.

FOODS

Tea: Put 1 sprig of young leaves in 1 pint of boiling water, cover, turn off the heat, and steep for 5 minutes. Remove the leaves, sweeten, and serve.

Cooked: Young leaves can be added to bean recipes to prevent gas, aid digestion, and improve flavor. Add 1 or 2 sprigs of fresh young leaves to a pot of cooking beans 3 or 4 minutes before the beans are ready to eat. Remove the epazote before serving.

Dried: The leaves can be dried and stored for future use. Dried, crumbled leaves can be used in place of fresh ones when cooking beans.

NO FUSS BEANS
Serves 6–8

1 pound red or pinto beans	12 ounces chunky salsa, hot
2 quarts water	1 teaspoon salt
6 ounces tomato sauce	2 sprigs epazote
Pinch of sugar	

Soak the beans overnight. Change the water to 2 quarts of fresh water. Cover the beans and boil them for 1 hour. Turn off the burner, but keep the lid on. After several hours, mix in all the other ingredients except the epazote. Cover and bring to a boil. Turn down the heat and simmer until the beans are cooked. Stir in the epazote and cook for 3 minutes more. Remove the epazote and serve the beans with hot corn tortillas and a green salad.

HORSETAIL

Equisetum arvense

Scouring Rush, Jointed Grass

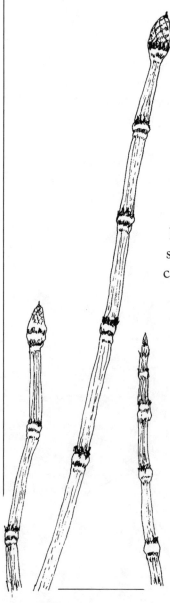

Features: Nonflowering horsetails are perennial, unbranched, rush-like herbs, which grow up to 3 feet high, have hollow stems, and grow from rootstocks. Their most distinctive feature is their ability to be separated at their nodes and put back together again, although once pulled apart, the sections above the separation are essentially dead. Horsetail stalks have deep vertical grooves, and feel rough and gritty. Almost unnoticeable, tiny, black, bristly, scale-like leaves hug the stems above the node lines. In spring, the stalk is crowned by a small, cone-like spike. Afterwards, the plant sends out fragile, feathery, pine needle-like branches that grow in whorled bands along the entire length of the stalk, making horsetail look like an entirely different plant. At this stage they resemble mare's tail, *Hippuris* spp., which is a perennial aquatic plant.

Facts: Horsetail grows in wet, moist, shaded locations throughout the world, except in Australia. Because they are coated with silica, horsetails can be used to scour pots and pans, file nails, and polish wood. They are high in calcium and can be used for food for both humans and animals, with limitations. Seventh-century Romans prepared young horsetails like asparagus and ate them. In Alaska, the Dena'ina collect the tubers after the snow melts and eat them raw or mixed with lard. The stems and leaves are burned to ashes, then the ashes are put on sores which have already been washed with horsetail tea. A tea made from the boiled shoots, fresh or ground, is drunk to treat high blood pressure, insomnia, nervous breakdown, and to purify the blood. In early spring, the entire stems and tuberous growths on the roots can be eaten, and during spring the piths can be eaten.

Warning: Horsetails contain aconitic acid, which is a nerve poison. Excessive consumption can cause sickness and mild poisoning.

FOODS

Tea: Put a few stems into a mug, add boiling water, cover, and steep for 5 minutes. Sweeten and serve.

Raw: The white pith of young stalks is tasty and can be eaten raw. Peel them first, and only eat the tender centers, not the tough outer stalks. In early spring, young tubers can be eaten raw or added to salads.

Cooked: Young stalks can be boiled, pickled, or steamed as a vegetable.

LABRADOR TEA

Ledum groenlandicum

Hudson Bay Tea, Marsh Tea, Moth Herb, Greenland Tea, Trapper's Tea

Features: Labrador tea is a sturdy, evergreen shrub which grows from 1 to 4 feet tall. Narrow-leaf Labrador tea, *Ledum decumbens*, is shorter, only growing from 1 to 2 feet tall. Both plants have Labrador tea's alternate, oval- to lance-shaped leaves, and small, fragrant, 5-petaled, white flowers. The flowers, which are borne in bouquet-like clusters at the tips of the branches, bloom from May to June. Easily recognized, Labrador tea's leathery little leaves are smooth on top and fuzzy underneath. This wool-like covering is initially grayish but becomes reddish-brown as the leaves age. The margins of the leaves are rolled inward, making the leaves appear narrower than they actually are. Labrador tea bushes are resinous, and the leaves are pleasantly aromatic when crushed. Because of their similar habitats, Labrador tea and toxic bog rosemary, *Andromeda polifolia*, are sometimes confused, despite the fact that bog rosemary has pale pink, bell-shaped flowers, and its leaves are not fuzzy.

Facts: Labrador tea grows in forest bogs and wet, peaty soil throughout Alaska, except for the Aleutians, in the northern part of North America, and in some mountain ranges farther south. Tea made from this bush is used to treat a variety of ailments. Janice J. Schofield of Alaska, author of *Discovering Wild Plants*, prefers to pick the green leaves and blossoms during summer but states that some people prefer to gather brown leaves in winter. In Alaska, the Dena'ina used Labrador tea both as tea and medicine. The Yup'ik drank the tea as a remedy for food poisoning and upset stomachs. Other people drank it to treat weak blood, colds, tuberculosis, arthritis, dizziness, heartburn, and stomach problems.

Warning: Labrador tea should be drunk in moderation by most people, and not consumed at all by people who have high blood pressure or a heart condition. The leaves contain a poisonous substance called ledol, which can cause cramping and paralysis.

FOODS

Tea: Thoroughly dry the leaves before using them. Then put 2 or 3 in a mug, fill with boiling water, cover, and steep for 5 to 10 minutes. Remove the leaves and serve hot or cold. Drink the tea in moderation since it is slightly laxative in nature. Labrador tea leaves can also be combined with other herbs for tea blends. In summer, the flowers can also be used to make tea.

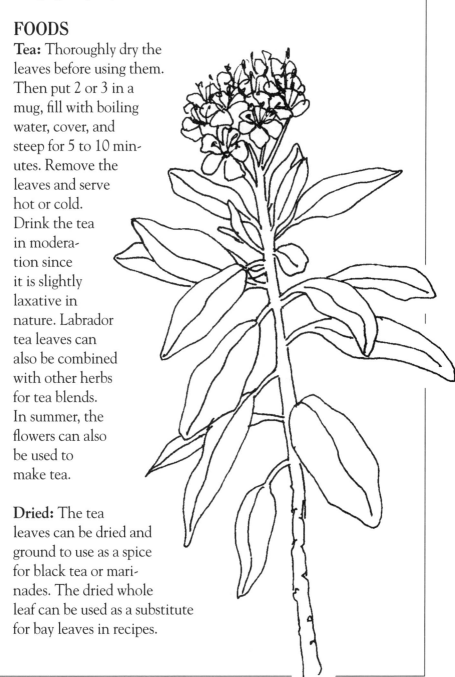

Dried: The tea leaves can be dried and ground to use as a spice for black tea or marinades. The dried whole leaf can be used as a substitute for bay leaves in recipes.

MUSHROOMS

There are three kinds of mushrooms: varieties that are usually edible, varieties that are sometimes edible, and those which are never edible. When collecting and eating mushrooms, you cannot be too careful. Some families have enjoyed hunting and eating wild mushrooms for generations and never had any trouble, while other mushroom enthusiasts have been less fortunate. As a precautionary measure, only distinctive, easily identified mushrooms are included in this book. It is up to you to ensure that any specimens you find are in good condition and growing in a nontoxic environment. Because some people are sensitive to mushrooms, it is always best to take a small taste initially to be sure that you and a specific variety are compatible. When gathering mushrooms, always keep the different varieties separate in case one of them is poisonous. Moreover, always cut a mushroom open before eating it. If it contains bugs or bug tunnels, do not eat it. Healthy mushroom flesh should be firm. If a mushroom passes all these tests, you are ready to move on to phase two, preparation. They keep best if you do not clean them until just before cooking. Although fresh mushrooms are always preferable, many varieties can be dried or frozen for future use. Mushrooms vary greatly in flavor and texture and considerably enhance most foods, so happy hunting.

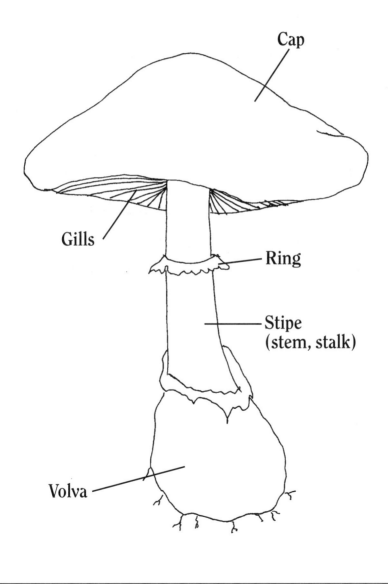

Cap

Gills

Ring

Stipe
(stem, stalk)

Volva

BLEWIT

Lepista nuda, Clitocybe nuda

Wood Blewit

Features: Blewits are striking purple mushrooms that grow in small communities in open fields hidden among leaves left over from autumn. In southern California they appear from fall until winter and are gone by the time the weather turns warm. They are sturdy with softly bulbous stalks and thick, broad, gently curved, smooth, sometimes moist caps. Growing under 3½ inches high, they are not large mushrooms, but their faded violet stalks and pale grayish or brownish-purple caps are truly eye-catching. Beneath the caps are buff- to violet-colored gills which sometimes extend all the way down to the tops of the stalks. The younger the mushroom is, the brighter its color and the more rounded its cap. The caps of older blewits begin to flatten, and the edges recede, revealing the gills beneath. Sometimes two or more of these mushrooms are joined at the base. Blewits have a subtle, pleasant fragrance and taste. Wood blewits and field blewits, *Lepista saeva*, are similar. However, young wood blewits are violet all over, whereas field blewits are pale brown with only a hint of purple. Fortunately, both are edible.

Facts: Blewits prefer slightly moist, shady locations under conifers, hardwood trees, or compost heaps and are widely distributed across the United States. The name blewit means "blue hat." Even though older blewits may fade to almost pale brown,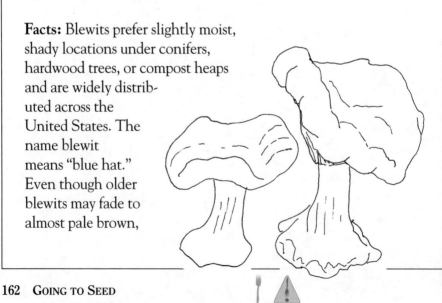

the gills and stalks usually retain their striking violet color. These mushrooms were sold commercially in Britain. The best time to collect blewits is in fall and winter. *Cortinarius violareus*, which can cause gastric upset when consumed, is sometimes mistaken for blewits because of its pale gills. However, blewits have stouter stalks which widen at the base, and they have white spores unlike *Cortinarius violareus*, which has brown spores. Also, blewits have smoother, shinier, browner caps which flatten out with age.

Warning: Some people are allergic to blewits. Only take a small taste at first and see how you react.

Warning: Do not eat Blewits raw.

FOODS
Cooked: Young blewits can be fried with onions, cooked with cream sauces, or added to soups, stews, tomato sauces, and omelettes.

BLEWIT OMELETTE
Serves 2

1 potato, diced	4 eggs, beaten
2 tablespoons butter	¼ cup milk
½ onion, diced	Salt and cayenne pepper
½ cup young blewits, cleaned and chopped	Parsley sprigs

Boil the potato in a little water until tender. Drain and set aside. Melt the butter in a frying pan. Sauté the onion until clear, then stir in the mushrooms. Meanwhile, beat the eggs and milk together. Add the potatoes to the mushrooms, then pour the egg mixture over all. Brown the eggs, flip, and brown the other side. Season to taste with salt and pepper and garnish with parsley.

BOLETE

Boletus spp.

Features: Boletes come in diverse sizes, shapes, and colors. Their distinguishing feature is a lack of gills. If you look under their thick-fleshed, well-rounded caps, you will find a sponge-like texture which resembles the inside of a cut-open English muffin. These mushrooms can be smaller than your hand or large enough to sit on. The stout stalks are usually smooth, and if you pull them out of the ground, you will often find that their bases are cup-shaped. The tops of these stalks fit snugly into a recessed place beneath the center of the caps. The caps range in color from pale gold to warm brown, and are sometimes red or a combination of hues. Most members of this family range from barely edible to simply delicious; however, a few varieties are poisonous. It is safest to avoid all specimens with red caps or whose flesh stains blue after being cut. They grow from July to September.

Facts: Like most mushrooms, boletes grow in shady, wooded areas, especially near pine or birch trees. They can be found throughout the northern temperate region of the United States, Europe, and Asia. One way to check if a bolete is edible is to make a spore print. Cut off the cap and place it spore-side down in such a manner that one half is on top of a white sheet of paper and the other half is on top of a black one. This way, if the spores are light they will show up on the black paper, and if they are dark they will show up on the light one. If you have a microscope, check if the spores are pink or red at their tips, and if so, do not eat the bolete.

Warning: There are many varieties of boletes; it is a good idea to look up those you collect in a definitive mushroom guide before eating them.

FOODS

Raw: Edible boletes can be eaten raw. They have a mild, pleasantly woody flavor.

Cooked: Edible boletes can be boiled, broiled, fried, stir-fried, added to sauces, or used in any recipe which calls for mushrooms.

MUSHROOM PIZZA

Serves 6

8 ounces tomato sauce	6 English muffins, halved
6 ounces tomato paste	1 cup mozzarella cheese, grated
¼ teaspoon oregano	¼ cup boletes, sliced
1 teaspoon basil	½ green pepper, chopped
¼ teaspoon thyme	¼ cup onions, chopped
Pinch of sugar	3 ounces sliced olives
	(optional)

Heat the tomato sauce, paste, and seasonings together. Spread the mixture over the cut English muffins. Top with cheese, mushrooms, green pepper, onions, and olives. Bake at 350 degrees for 10 minutes or until done.

INKY CAP

Coprinus atramentarius

Common Inky Cap, Common Ink Cap

Features: It is a real feat to find an inky cap still young enough to eat. On a walk you may spot a few of these small, delicate mushrooms huddled together on a tree root, but by the time you return, their caps may have already started dissolving into a black, ink-like puddle of liquefied spores. Inky caps have slightly gray-brown, scaly, at first egg-shaped then bell-shaped caps which grow 1 to 2 inches in diameter. Once they mature, these caps experience major meltdown, dissolving from their margins inward as they release their spores. They become shapeless, with tatters of the remaining cap hanging despondently down over their smooth, slender, white, spindle-shaped stalk. These stalks grow up to 3 inches tall, are hollow, and have a delicate ring near their bases. Mica cap (*Coprinus micaceus*), also known as inky cap, is very similar but has shiny particles on its cap which are washed away by the rain. These caps are deeply striated and look as if they were pleated.

Facts: Inky caps grow in grassy areas and on rotted wood and buried tree stumps throughout North America. Some varieties of inky cap contain a chemical which does not mix well with alcohol, and consuming both at the same time can make you extremely sick. Antabuse, a medicine used in the treatment of alcoholics, has similar properties. Recovering alcoholics take this medicine regularly, and if they drink alcohol, the antabuse kicks in, and they soon regret their indiscretion. If you want to eat food containing inky caps and drink alcohol without getting sick, wait ½ hour after drinking an alcoholic beverage before consuming inky caps; and after consuming inky caps, wait 1 to 2 days before you drink alcohol. These mushrooms are available from spring until the first winter frost.

Warning: Drinking alcohol and eating inky caps at the same time can cause extreme illness.

FOODS

Raw: Inky caps are edible raw, and they taste good.

Cooked: They can be used in all recipes calling for mushrooms, except those which call for alcohol.

SPAGHETTI WITH MUSHROOM SAUCE
Serves 4–6

8 ounces spaghetti	12 ounces tomato purée
1 tablespoon olive oil	½ cup water
2 cloves garlic, minced	Pinch of sugar
1 onion, chopped	1 teaspoon oregano
½ cup inky caps, cleaned and sliced	4 fresh basil leaves, chopped
½ red pepper, chopped	Salt and cayenne pepper
2 ounces tomato paste	Parmesan cheese

Add the spaghetti to boiling water and cook, uncovered, until done. Meanwhile, heat the olive oil in a deep frying pan. Sauté the garlic and onion until clear. Stir in the mushrooms and red pepper, then add the tomato paste and tomato purée. Add the water until you have the desired consistency. Then stir in the sugar and spices. Bring to a boil, cover, and lower the heat. Simmer for several hours over a low heat, stirring often, and adding water as needed. Drain the spaghetti and serve with the sauce and Parmesan cheese. Accompany it with garlic bread and a green salad.

MOREL

Morchella esculenta

Yellow Morel, Blond Morel,
Honeycomb Morel, Sponge Mushroom

Features: Morels have short stems and long, distinctive caps which are both deeply ridged and pitted. The caps of *Morchella esculenta* are tannish-brown, and their stalks are almost white. These stalks are hollow, growing from ½ to 1 inch in diameter. The caps, which are also hollow, grow from 2 to 7¾ inches in height. An average morel is 5 inches tall, the cap 3 inches and the stalk 2. Morels, which do not have rings, begin to appear around May. Although these mushrooms are unusual, they are not entirely unique. Imposters known as false morels, *Gyromitra* spp., also have long, deeply ridged, pitted caps. But their caps have a squashed, misshapen appearance, and the shapes of their pits are very irregular, whereas the elegant morel has pits with clear borders and a vertical motif. If you cut open the stalks of these two mushrooms, it is apparent that false morel's stalk is chambered, whereas the real morel's is hollow and empty. It is necessary to recognize these differences because false morels contain a cumulative toxin which can prove deadly, whereas the real morels are edible.

Facts: Morels are widely distributed throughout North America, growing in orchards, woods, gardens, clearings, and especially burned-over ground. They are extremely difficult to grow commercially and are priced accordingly. The best time to collect them is during spring.

Warning: Morels may cause stomach upset if consumed with alcohol. It is not advisable to eat them raw.

FOODS

Cooked: Morels can be used in any mushroom recipes which do not include alcohol. Because the entire mushroom is hollow, it can be stuffed and baked. Be sure to clean them thoroughly before cooking.

Dried: If you are fortunate enough to find more morels than you can eat, the extras can be dried and stored for future use.

SAUTÉED MUSHROOMS ON TOAST
Serves 4

    4 tablespoons butter
    ½ pound fresh morels, cleaned and sliced lengthwise
    Salt
    8 slices toast

Melt the butter in a frying pan over a medium temperature, being careful not to brown it, then turn down the heat. Add the mushrooms and sauté them until they are tender. Season them with salt if desired and serve immediately over hot toast. Morels cooked in cream sauce are good, too.

OYSTER MUSHROOM

Pleurotus cornucopiae

Features: Although they are considered mushrooms, I think of oyster mushrooms more as a shelf fungus, because they always grow in tiers on trees and dead timber. Some varieties have short, inconspicuous stalks, whereas others have none at all. When there are stalks, they are often fused together in bunches. *Pleurotus cornucopiae*, the species pictured, does have a short stalk. Oyster mushrooms always grow in families of overlapping individual mushrooms. They have smooth, graceful, rounded caps which range in color from almost white to brown or pale brownish-lavender. Initially, these caps are pale tan but darken as they mature. They range from fan-shaped to shallowly funneled, or a combination. The gills beneath the caps are creamy white, crowded, deep, and continuous. As the caps age, their smooth margins become ruffled or fluted with tiny splits. In summer, the caps tend to be flat, whitish, and fan-shaped, but in winter they are darker and more rounded. Their thick flesh has a pleasant odor. Oyster mushroom caps usually grow from 2 to 4¾ inches in diameter, and their spore print is lilac.

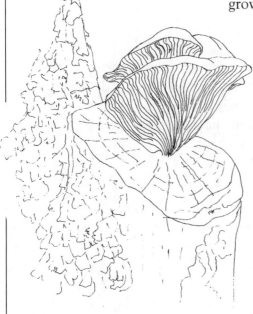

Facts: Oyster mushrooms grow throughout the United States on trees and dead timber in forested areas. These attractive mushrooms are usually available year-round, although the best season to collect them is from late summer through late fall until the first frost. Occasionally they are available in supermarkets. As their name implies, oyster mush-rooms taste like oysters, especially when they are cooked. They should always be eaten when they are young, since older specimens are tough.

FOODS
Cooked: Oyster mushrooms taste best when cooked. Because their flesh is thick, they can be cut in pieces and used as you would oysters or chicken.

OYSTER CHOWDER
Serves 2

1 tablespoon butter	½ cup celery, sliced
¾ cup oyster mushrooms, diced	1 potato, cubed
	¾ cup milk
¾ cup water	Salt and cayenne pepper

Melt the butter and sauté the mushrooms until they are soft. Add the water and bring to a boil. Then add the celery and potato. Cover and cook over a medium temperature for about 15 min-utes—until the potato is done. Add the milk and heat but do not boil. Season to taste with salt and pepper, and serve with hot sourdough bread.

PUFFBALL

Lycoperdon spp.

Features: Puffballs come in a wide variety of sizes and shapes, from as small as a gumball to as large as a watermelon. They are basically spherical in shape, and most varieties have a smooth white surface. A few of the species have a tiny stalk, or a stalk-like base, but most just sit on the ground. Puffballs have no caps or gills. They are rounded, and if you cut them open, young, healthy specimens are soft and white inside, almost like marshmallows. When they mature and prepare to release their spores, they become dark inside. Because they resemble rocks, small puffballs are often easy to overlook, but it is hard to miss the larger ones, especially when they can grow up to 24 inches in diameter. Their odor is earthy and pleasant.

Facts: Puffballs grow almost everywhere there is rich, moist soil. They are common in the United States, especially in the eastern and central states. Early summer to late autumn is the best time to find them. It is relatively easy to determine if a puffball is edible by cutting it open. A healthy puffball has firm but soft, unblemished, white flesh. If it is dark, blotchy, or discolored, do not eat it since it is spoiled. If you cut a specimen open and see what appears to be the silhouette of a mushroom inside, throw it away. It is not a puffball but an immature amanita, and most amanitas are deadly poisonous. There is also a poisonous puffball, *Scleroderma citrinum*, which is not white like the edible varieties but yellow-brown, with a small, round base and lines, cracks, and raised warts on its surface. Once you have established that you have a healthy, edible puffball, eat it while it is still fresh. Native Americans used puffballs for both food and medicine. For medicinal purposes, they dried and powdered puffballs, then used the powder to treat broken eardrums. To stop bleeding, they sprinkled wounds with puffball spores. Puffballs contain a tiny amount of calvacin, which is said to inhibit cancer cells.

FOODS

Raw: Puffballs can be eaten raw. They have a pleasant texture and an agreeable flavor.

Cooked: After the base is cut off and the skin peeled, puffballs can be used in any recipe calling for mushrooms. In fact, my family and I prefer them to other mushrooms because of their flavor and texture.

Dried: Puffballs can be dried or frozen. Slice them into thin pieces and dry them, or sauté them in butter or olive oil and then freeze them.

PUFFBALLS WITH SOUR CREAM
Serves 2

1 tablespoon butter	¾ cup sour cream
½ medium onion, chopped	Salt
1 cup puffballs, sliced	4 slices sourdough toast

Melt the butter and sauté the onion until clear. Stir in the puffball slices and gently sauté them over medium heat until they are coated with butter. Stir in the sour cream and simmer until warm. Season to taste with salt and serve immediately over hot toast.

CREAM OF PUFFBALL SOUP
Serves 4–6

2 tablespoons butter	4 cups chicken broth
1 onion, chopped	2 cups milk
1 cup puffballs, sliced	1 teaspoon thyme
6–8 small potatoes, cubed	Salt and cayenne pepper

Melt the butter and sauté the onion until clear. Stir in the puffball slices. Then add the potatoes and chicken broth. Cover and bring to a boil. Lower the heat and continue cooking until the potatoes are tender, about 15 minutes. Add the milk and thyme. Heat but do not boil. Season to taste with salt and pepper and serve.

SHAGGY MANE

Coprinus comatus

Lawyer's Wig, Ink Caps, Shaggy Inky Cap

Features: This is one of the inky caps which releases its spores by dissolving its cap from the margin inward, leaving shreddy remnants and a black puddle below. However, before its decline it is an impressive white mushroom which can grow up to 13 inches in height, although the norm is closer to 6 inches. A great deal of the shaggy mane's height is its tall cap, which is almost egg-shaped at first but becomes progressively more parasol-shaped as it matures. These caps are a lovely, pristine white, with an interesting shaggy surface of small, fluffy scales, which resemble the curls on the old-fashioned powdered wigs worn by English lawyers. The stalks are hollow, and there is a thin ring located just below the base of the cap. Young, firm shaggy manes are delicious. Once you pick them, do not wait before you cook them, or you may end up with a puddle of ink instead of a tasty treat.

Facts: Shaggy manes can be found growing on newly turned soil in gardens and meadows, in garbage dumps, and landfills throughout America. They are most evident over summer. Shaggy manes and the other inky caps were actually used as a source of ink by settlers, who boiled the mature mushrooms, strained the resulting fluid, then added a special ingredient to prevent the ink from molding. Shaggy manes do not mix well with alcohol, and the combination will make you ill. Thus avoid using them in any recipes that call for wine.

Warning: Eating shaggy manes and drinking alcohol at the same time can cause illness.

FOODS

Cooked: Young shaggy manes are mild and pleasant-flavored when cooked. They make a great soup when combined with butter, onions, and potatoes.

BEEF STROGANOFF
Serves 4

1 tablespoon butter	1 tablespoon tomato paste
2 cloves garlic, minced	1 tablespoon butter
½ onion, minced	3–4 young shaggy manes
1⅓ pounds lean meat, cut in strips	1 tablespoon butter
	3 tablespoons flour
1 cup water	1 cup sour cream

Melt 1 tablespoon of butter and sauté the garlic and onion until clear. Add the meat and brown. Mix in the water and tomato paste. Cover and bring to a boil. Lower the heat and simmer for 30 minutes, stirring occasionally. In a separate pan, melt 1 tablespoon butter and sauté the mushrooms. Remove the mushrooms and melt the rest of the butter, using the same pan. Lower the heat to moderate and slowly stir in the flour. Gradually add liquid from the meat. Stir until thickened, then add all the remaining meat, gravy, and mushrooms. When everything is well blended, stir in the sour cream and serve over egg noodles, rice, kasha, or baked potatoes.

SULFUR SHELF

Laetiporus sulphureus

Chicken Mushroom

Features: Consider yourself fortunate if you find young, yellow or bright orange sulfur shelf fungus, which grows in attractive, velvety, overlapping bracts on trees and tree stumps. They begin appearing in late spring, when the young bracts are somewhat lumpy and lemon-colored. They become orange as they mature, and the bracts begin to fan out, growing up to 12 inches in diameter. Beneath these bracts are bright sulfur yellow-colored pores. Older sulfur shelves are often decorated with attractive, concentric bands of yellow, warm orange, and a darker russet color. The edge of each bract is also russet-colored. Sulfur shelf is usually stalkless and has no gills. It is sometimes confused with jack-o'-lantern fungus, *Omphalotus illudens*, which is poisonous. However, although jack-o'-lantern fungus is orange, it has no striations of color, its surface is shiny, it glows in the dark, and the individual mushrooms have stems. They appear to form bracts because they overlap.

Facts: Sulfur shelf grows in late spring on trees and dead wood in forested areas. This fungus is unusual in both its appearance and its chicken-like flavor. Although sulfur shelf, especially the young, tender tips, is edible, except when growing on eucalyptus trees, some people may be sensitive to it.

Warning: When sulfur shelf grows on eucalyptus trees, it is no longer edible. It can cause painful gastronomic upset within an hour or so after consumption. This fact clarifies the warning contained in some books stating that sulfur shelf grown in California is poisonous. To my knowledge, it is only inedible when growing on eucalyptus trees.

FOODS

Raw: Only the young sulfur shelf, which are usually available from late spring through early autumn, should be eaten. Cut them into bite-sized pieces and use them for a chicken-flavored snack.

Cooked: Sulfur shelf does not have much flavor until it is cooked. It can be shredded before cooking for a chicken-like texture, and a little paprika can be sprinkled over it for added color. Cook sulfur shelf as you would any other mushroom.

Dried/Frozen: This firm fungus is suitable for drying or freezing.

MARINATED AND BROILED SULFUR SHELF FUNGUS WITH FLANK STEAK

This recipe is adapted from *The Wild Gourmet* by Babette Brackett and Maryanne Lash.

Serves 4

1 tablespoon brown sugar	3 cloves garlic, minced
2 tablespoons olive oil	½ teaspoon fresh ginger,
¼ cup soy sauce	grated, or 1 teaspoon
¼ cup water	powdered
½ cup merlot wine	2 cups sulfur shelf,
3 juniper berries,	cut in strips
lightly crushed	1½ pounds flank steak
	(optional)

Combine the first 8 ingredients and pour the resulting marinade over the sulfur shelf and steak. Marinate for at least 6 hours, turning the meat every hour. Then broil the fungus and meat for 4 to 6 minutes on each side. If you are only broiling the sulfur shelf, 3 to 4 minutes on each side will suffice. This is delicious served with a crisp salad, crusty bread, and some tender pasta.

NIGHTSHADE (WHITE-FLOWERED)

Solanum douglasii

Western Black Nightshade

Features: There are over 100 different species in this genus. Western black nightshade is a common, native, perennial herb. Blooming from February through March, **its white flowers appear to have 5 petals—all attached at their base. Each flower has a central cone of beak-like, yellow anthers.** This nightshade is many-branched and spreading, and can grow up to 4 feet tall and 3 feet wide. Despite its size, it is a delicate, almost vine-like plant with stalks which are covered with a fine white fuzz. Ovate, dark green nightshade leaves come to a point at the tip, and their generally smooth margins are sometimes irregularly toothed. Nightshade berries are about the size of a small pea and are deep purple-black when mature. **Because edible black nightshade berries are very similar to the berries of poisonous purple nightshade, *Solanum xantii*, it is important to distinguish between them. The berries of purple nightshade are smaller and purplish when ripe. Its flowers are red-violet, and consist of a single, circular blossom as opposed to individual petals. Do not pick the berries unless there are flowers present; this way you can be sure which variety of nightshade you have.**

Facts: Western black nightshade grows in coastal sage, on partially shaded slopes, and in canyons at elevations under 5,000 feet. **Although fully ripe western black nightshade berries are edible, the unripe ones are not, nor is any other part of the plant edible since it contains solanin, which is a poisonous substance.** Consumption of large quantities of raw leaves or green berries will cause convulsions, delirium, rapid pulse rate, cramps, and sometimes death. **Even people who enjoy eating the ripe berries raw often take the precaution of cooking them for a few minutes first.** Most of these berries are ripe by late summer, and some are available into autumn. Native Americans used the juice

Bold Face type is to emphasize safety considerations

from the fully ripe berries as medicine to cure sore throats, pink-eye, and eyestrain; it was even squeezed directly into the eye. Western black nightshade berry juice is reputed to improve the vision of older people. The fresh leaves were crushed and used as an antiseptic on wounds and skin problems.

Warning: Eat only the ripe berries of western black nightshade; the unripe berries and other parts of the plant contain solanin, a poisonous substance that can cause convulsions, delirium, rapid pulse rate, cramps, or death.

FOODS

Raw: Although many people eat the fully ripe, tomato-like berries raw with no harmful results, do not eat the green berries raw. Most people feel safer eating the berries if they are cooked.

Cooked: The berries can be used to make jams, jellies, and sauces. A few brave souls eat the young leaves but only after they have been boiled in 2 changes of water and the water has been discarded.

BERRY GOOD JAM

Makes 3 pints
    4 cups of fully ripe berries
    2 tablespoons lemon juice
    4 cups sugar
    1 box pectin

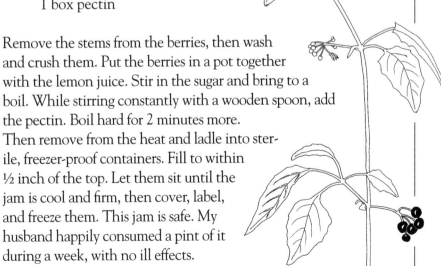

Remove the stems from the berries, then wash and crush them. Put the berries in a pot together with the lemon juice. Stir in the sugar and bring to a boil. While stirring constantly with a wooden spoon, add the pectin. Boil hard for 2 minutes more. Then remove from the heat and ladle into sterile, freezer-proof containers. Fill to within ½ inch of the top. Let them sit until the jam is cool and firm, then cover, label, and freeze them. This jam is safe. My husband happily consumed a pint of it during a week, with no ill effects.

PENNYROYAL

Monardella odoratissima

Mountain Pennyroyal, Coyote Mint

Features: Pennyroyal is a short member of the mint family which usually grows about 6 to 14 inches high. It is a delicate, slightly branched perennial which flowers in late summer. It has a square stem and opposite pairs of leaves. The reddish stem is dusted with white, and is often gritty near its base. From late summer into early autumn wonderfully fragrant, pale to bright purple flowers gather loosely together to form flowerheads at the top of the stem and branches. All of the flowers do not bloom at the same time, so some of the flowerheads appear fuller than others. Pennyroyal occasionally resembles a miniature candelabra when its fragile branches curve upward on either side of the main stem. At the intersection of each branch and the main stem is a leaf. Its small, green, lanceolate leaves have smooth margins, are green on both sides, and are covered on both sides with barely discernible short hairs. Initially, these leaves stick out almost horizontally from the plant, but as they get older they begin to droop. All parts of the plant are intensely aromatic, and they retain their odor for years. If you touch any part, the scent will linger on your hand.

Facts: Striking pennyroyal plants can be found growing on dry chaparral slopes throughout the United States, especially in the Northwest and the East. There is a difference of opinion about whether this plant, *Monardella ordoratissima*, should be classified as a pennyroyal, or if it should be known only as coyote mint; it is now classified under both names. Because fleas cannot stand pennyroyal, it is an important ingredient for flea collars. It also makes a great sachet. Pennyroyal has been used medicinally by many Native American people. Miwoks made a tea from the stems and flowerheads, which they drank to relieve colds and fevers. Other groups, including Californios, made a similar tea from mustang mint, *Monardella lanceolata*. Their name for this mint is *poleo*. An infusion made from the leaves of "true pennyroyal," *Mentha pulegium*, was taken to improve digestion, relieve flatulence, and treat bronchial ailments. Many species of pennyroyal are on the rare and endangered plants list, so be careful what you pick, and only take as much as you need. I prefer to collect pennyroyal in late summer or early autumn when it is flowering.

Warning: Pennyroyal contains a volatile oil called pulegone, which can be toxic if consumed in large quantities. Pennyroyal tea should never be drunk by pregnant women, and it should only be used in moderation by everyone else.

FOODS

Tea: Put 1 sprig in a teapot, add boiling water, cover, and steep for 5 minutes. One small sprig will generally suffice for 2 cups of tea. Pennyroyal tea not only tastes delicious, but it also smells incredibly good. Never boil pennyroyal, or it will lose its flavor.

POKEWEED

Phytolacca americana

Poke, Pigeon Berry, Red-Ink Plant, Inkberry

Features: A truly magnificent plant, prolific pokeweed grows from a few hesitant leaves to a showy perennial shrub 10 to 12 feet high in a matter of weeks. At first, there is an upright cluster of several large, thick, crisp, oval leaves which have slightly ruffled margins. Often these leaves are curled together, unfurling as they mature. The leaves, which are small enough to eat one day, may be too large and mature the next. Then a smooth, stout, yellow-green stalk emerges, putting out branches as it grows. Its flowers are small and inconspicuous, with 5 tiny white or green petals. They are followed by racemes of flattened inkberries growing at the tips of the branches. Meanwhile, the stalk turns a lovely shade of bright red-violet. The color of the berries changes from green to red-violet before they ripen and turn a purplish-black— a process that occurs very quickly. Pokeweed is characterized by a strong, unpleasant odor when broken. It spreads by rhizomes, and this year's solitary plant will be part of a thriving community by the next year. There are 25 species in this genus.

Facts: Hardy pokeweed grows in rich, well-drained soil in fields, along roadsides, on open ground, and at the edge of woods. It is common throughout most of the United States except in the Northwest and north-central region. All parts of pokeweed are considered poisonous except for the young shoots and leaves. Young leaves are usually available in spring but may appear later. They should only be eaten if they are under 8 inches tall, bundled together or spread out, and cooked. The Chinese boiled the leaves and ate them. Some people believe the berries are edible, and cook them into pies and jellies or use them as a food coloring. The berries can also be made into a passable ink. Native Americans dried the roots and berries to use them, in moderation, as a purgative. The roots were utilized to treat rheumatism and glandular swellings. Pokeweed shoots are rich in vitamins A and C.

Warning: Raw or undercooked roots and the mature plant all contain an alkaloid called phytolaccine, which is a drastic purgative. They also contain saponin, which is considered poisonous. If you have any cuts, it is best to wear gloves when collecting pokeweed because its poisonous compounds can be absorbed through open wounds and are harmful to your blood.

FOODS

Cooked: Never eat raw pokeweed! Pick only young shoots and leaves which are 6 to 8 inches tall. The leaves should either be folded up or relaxed outward, and the shoots should still be green. Cut them off 1 inch above the ground, boil them for 10 minutes in a little water, drain off the water, then boil them again, this time for 20 or 30 minutes. Pokeweed greens are delicious served with butter and salt. The young shoots can be dipped in batter and fried.

Frozen: Peel the young stalks and cut them into 4-inch segments. Blanch them for 3 minutes in boiling water, and dip them in cold water. Then drain, package, and freeze them.

POKEWEED SOUFFLÉ
Serves 4–6

3 cups young pokeweed leaves and shoots, chopped	¾ cup mozzarella cheese
2 tablespoons butter	Salt and cayenne pepper
3 tablespoons flour	3 eggs, beaten
¾ cup milk	Parmesan cheese

Boil the pokeweed for 15 minutes. Drain and put in a baking pan. Melt the butter, blend in the flour, and add the milk. When the sauce is smooth, stir in the mozzarella cheese and season to taste with salt and pepper. Add the eggs to the sauce and pour it over the pokeweed. Top with Parmesan cheese. Bake at 400 degrees for about 20 minutes or until done.

PYRACANTHA

Pyracantha coccinea

Firethorn

Features: Pyracantha is a bushy little evergreen shrub which grows up to 6½ feet high and comes from southern Europe and Asia Minor. It has grayish-brown bark, and its many branches are covered with narrow, glossy green leaves which are elliptical in shape and have finely toothed margins. From March through April, numerous small, white, 5-petaled flowers appear growing in compact clusters along the branches. Dense hanging bunches of bright, eye-catching orange to red, pea-sized berries follow. In spring, often some of last year's berries still remain on the bush when the flowers bloom.

Facts: Pyracantha berries are available almost year-round, with new ones appearing from late summer through autumn. Although they are not particularly tasty, pyracantha berries are edible, but only after they are cooked. Raw pyracantha berries contain volatile cyanogens and have been implicated in the poisoning of children in England; cooking removes these cyanogens. Pyracantha branches are a popular Christmas decoration because they have evergreen leaves and attractive red berries. These shrubs are also often used to brighten the divider strips of highways, sometimes with unexpected results. Pyracantha berries which are past their prime ferment, and birds that eat them sometimes become drunk! Then they fly around erratically, which is hazardous for drivers and often fatal for the birds. For this reason, many cities have removed these dangerous plants from their roads.

Warning: Since pyracantha is usually a domestic plant, it is important to verify it has not been sprayed with chemicals before you eat the berries. Pyracantha berries must be cooked to remove cyanogens.

FOODS

Cooked: The ripe berries can be cooked and made into sauces, jellies, and marmalades.

OUTRAGEOUS ORANGE-PYRACANTHA MARMALADE

Makes approximately 1 ½ cups

2 cups pyracantha berries, cleaned
1 cup water
Dash salt
1 orange, including grated peel, juice, and pulp

1 lemon, juiced
½ teaspoon allspice
½ teaspoon cinnamon
½ cup sugar
3 tablespoons cornstarch

Put the berries, water, and salt in a pot. Simmer for 10 minutes. Strain the berries through a sieve, retaining as much liquid as possible. Put the juice and all the remaining ingredients except the cornstarch in the pot. Simmer until the orange peel is tender, about 30 minutes. Then remove a few tablespoonfuls of the warm liquid and mix it with the cornstarch. Add this mixture to the juice, and continue stirring and simmering until thickened. Pour into sterile containers. Cool and refrigerate.

WILD PEONY

Paeonia californica

California Peony, Western Peony, Coastal Peony

Features: A truly unique plant, wild peony is a perennial which grows 1 to 2 feet tall and 2 to 3 feet in diameter, in bushy clusters. The large, pinnately divided leaves are at least twice divided and grow alternately along the stalk and branches. The stout, erect flower stalks each bear a single flower. These large, hanging flowers always appear as if they are not quite open. They have 5 to 6 deep blackish-red petals and may bloom as soon as late January after an early rain. By April, the flowers are replaced by large, fleshy, capsule-like fruits which hang down to the ground, although wild peonies growing up north may bloom as late as July.

Facts: Wild peony can be found growing along dry canyons and waste places from central California to Mexico, and north to Washington, Wyoming, and Idaho. The best time to collect the leaves is early in spring before the plants blossom. In the past, wild peony has been used medicinally, especially its roots. It was brewed into a tea by

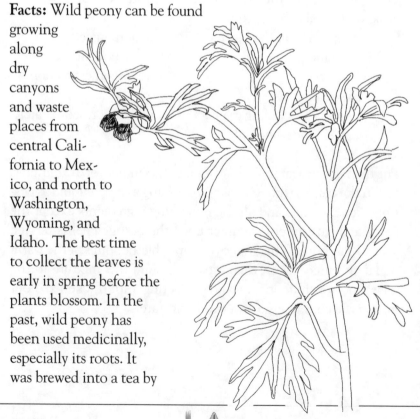

steeping ½ teaspoon of chopped root in a cup of boiling water. This tea was drunk to relieve melancholia and certain types of stress. Californios used raw wild peony root as a remedy for stomach complaints, and Native Americans made a drink from the powdered roots, which was used as a remedy for colds and sore throats. Root tea was also utilized to treat cramps, muscle pains, shaking, and coughs. Paiutes made their cough medicine from the seeds. After much effort, Kumeyiis were able to eat the young leaves. First the leaves were boiled, then put into a cloth sack. Next stones were added to the sack as ballast, and it was set overnight in a running stream so the water would leach the bitterness from the leaves. Then the leaves were cooked, sometimes as a vegetable with onions; other times they were added to cornmeal mush.

Warning: Without proper preparation, consumption of wild peony causes nausea. Pregnant women should not eat it or drink tea made from it.

FOODS

Tea: First slice the roots horizontally and place them in an oven to brown. Then take 2 or 3 slices and boil them in 1 quart of water until the water becomes colored. This tea is said to be good for indigestion.

Cooked: Do not eat the leaves raw, and only cook young leaves gathered before the flower stalks appear. Boil the leaves in several changes of water, until they no longer taste bitter. Then cook them with onions or use them in a stir-fry.